NATIVE AMERICANS

AN INSIDE LOOK AT THE TRIBES
AND TRADITIONS

19

NATIVE AMERICANS

AN INSIDE LOOK AT THE TRIBES
AND TRADITIONS

By
Laura Buller

Consultant
Dr Darren Ranco

A Dorling Kindersley Book

Dorling **DK** Kindersley

LONDON, NEW YORK, SYDNEY, DELHI,
PARIS, MUNICH, and JOHANNESBURG

Project Editor Emma Johnson
Project Art Editor James Marks
Senior Editor Fran Jones
Senior Art Editor Marcus James
Category Publisher Jayne Parsons
Managing Art Editor Jacquie Gulliver
Picture Researcher Angela Anderson
Production Erica Rosen
DTP Designers Matthew Ibbotson and Louise Paddick

First published in Great Britain in 2001 by
Dorling Kindersley Limited
80 Strand
London WC2R 0RL

2 4 6 8 10 9 7 5 3 1

The CIP Catalogue record for this book is available
from the British Library

ISBN 0-7513-3082-5

Reproduced by Colourscan, Singapore
Printed and bound by L.E.G.O., Italy

See our complete
catalogue at
www.dk.com

Note to Parents

Every effort has been made to ensure that the information in this book is as up-to-date
as possible at the time of going to press. The internet, by its very nature, is liable to
change. Homepages and website content is constantly being updated, as well as website
addresses. In addition, websites may contain material or links to material that may be
unsuitable for children. The publishers, therefore, cannot accept responsibility for any
third party websites or any material contained in or linked to the same or for any
consequences arising from use of the internet; nor can the publishers guarantee that any
website or urls featured in this book will be as shown. Parents are strongly advised to
ensure that access to the internet by children is supervised by a responsible adult.

Reading Borough Libraries
0118 901 5950

Self Service Receipt for Borrowing

Name: 24126001948327

Title: Native Americans : an inside look at t
tribes and traditions

Item: 34126000187750

Due Back: 24/08/2023

Total Borrowing: 1
03/08/2023 13:38:30

Thank you for using the library.

For renewals visit
www.reading.gov.uk/libraries

CONTENTS

6
INTRODUCTION

8
WHO ARE THE
NATIVE AMERICANS?

14
SPIRIT WORLD

18
MEET THE FAMILY

26
DAILY LIFE

34
WAR CRIES AND
PEACE PIPES

38
ARTS AND CRAFTS

44
PEOPLE OF THE
WOODLANDS

50
PEOPLE OF THE
SOUTHEAST

54
BUFFALO HUNTERS

60
THE SURVIVORS

64
HIGH PLATEAU

68
DESERT DWELLERS

74
THE WEST COASTERS

78
TOTEM TRIBES

82
THE FROZEN NORTH

85
REFERENCE SECTION

94
INDEX

96
CREDITS

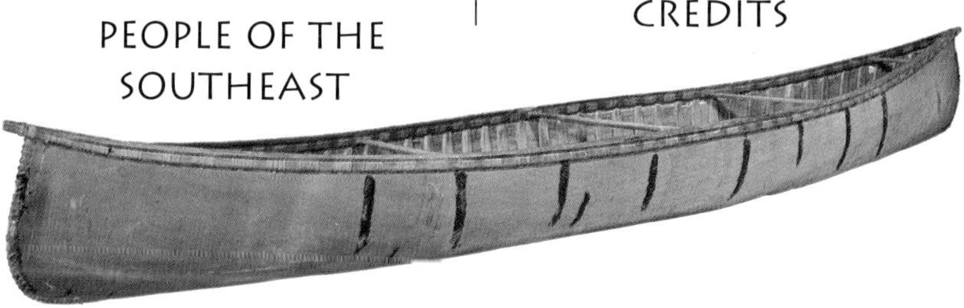

INTRODUCTION

Imagine you are a European explorer, sent by your country across the ocean in search of the legendary treasures of the New World – North America. At journey's end, you proudly plant your nation's flag and boldly claim the land as yours – only to be greeted by a group of people who seem to be saying "And who are you?"

For North America was hardly a new world. Before Europeans arrived, it had been settled for at least 30,000 years. And it wasn't exactly up for grabs. It was already home to a diverse

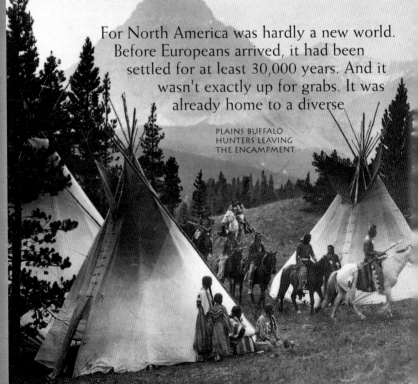

PLAINS BUFFALO
HUNTERS LEAVING
THE ENCAMPMENT

group of people who had adapted to – and thrived in – all sorts of ways of life. We now know these people as Native Americans. This book is all about their lives, their history, and their culture.

Firstly you'll be introduced to some customs, beliefs, and ideas that shaped the world of Native Americans. Explore tribal dwellings, from snow houses to desert tower blocks. See how the daily search for food dominated lives, and how many tribes survived the unsurvivable. Learn about traditional arts and crafts, rituals that marked each new season, and the sacred power of the spirit world.

It's wrong to generalize when talking about people who belonged to at least 300 different tribes. That's why the second part of the book covers the tribes region by region – people who lived in the same area usually had a similar way of life. You'll meet the totem pole carvers of the Pacific Northwest, the Great Plains buffalo hunters, and the Californian hunter-gatherers, amongst others.

Although much of this information tells you how Native Americans used to live, they are still a vital part of North American culture today.

For those of you who want to explore the subject in more detail – and to connect with modern Native American life – there are black Log On "bites" throughout the book. These will direct you to some websites where you can discover more about the tribes and traditions of Native Americans.

WHO ARE THE NATIVE AMERICANS?

Tens of thousands of years ago, bands of hunters crossed a frozen land bridge from Asia to coldly go where no man or woman had gone before – the Americas. Over centuries, the descendants of these first Americans spread across the continent, from Alaska to South America. By the time European explorers "discovered" the New World in 1492, there were more than a million people living in North America alone, divided into some 300 tribes. Each had its own legends, customs, language, and way of life. These people are the Native Americans.

PATHWAYS FROM ASIA TO NORTH AMERICA

A cross the bridge

We don't know exactly when – or just how – the first Americans arrived, but most scientists think that it was sometime during the last Ice Age, which chilled the Earth from about 35,000 to 10,000 years ago. Vast sheets of ice called glaciers – some a mile high – covered much of the northern lands. Because the glaciers locked up so much ocean water, Ice Age seas were smaller and lower, and much of

ANCIENT HUNTERS LURED MAMMOTHS INTO BRUSH-COVERED PITS, THEN HURLED HEAVY STONES ON THEIR PREY.

STONE WEAPON POINTS
SHAPED BY ICE AGE
HUNTERS MORE THAN
10,000 YEARS AGO.

the land that is now submerged
was dry. For instance, the
80-km (50-mile) gap between
Siberia and Alaska is now
underwater. But during the Ice
Age, dry land connected the
two continents, providing a
dry crosswalk.

A mammoth task

The first people to trek across
to America were probably not
looking for a new home or a
big adventure – they just
wanted something to eat. That
something was a huge, woolly
elephant called a mammoth.
Just one of these long-tusked
beasts would provide a winter's
worth of food, a wardrobe of
warm fur clothing, and even
shelter – a framework of
mammoth bones draped in
fur. If the mammoth got away,
there were literally tonnes of
other out-sized creatures to
hunt, from sabre-toothed tigers

to bear-sized beavers. The hunters were armed with rocks shaped and sharpened into knives, arrowheads, and spear points to stab, slice, and dice their gigantic prey.

Continental drift

The hunting was good in the new land, and so was the gathering – there were plenty of plants, seeds, shellfish, and wild berries to eat between mammoths. Steady streams of peckish people continued to cross into North America. Some stayed on the move, following their furry food sources from one place to another. They developed better weapons and designed houses that they could pack up and take away. Still others ventured beyond the ice to the western part of the continent, where food was so plentiful they

THE ANASAZI PEOPLE MADE MULTI-STOREY HOMES UNDER THE OVERHANGING ROCK IN THIS CLIFF DWELLING FROM 1000 BC.

11

decided to settle. They learned how to grow crops (especially corn), make pottery and weave baskets, build more permanent houses, and set up a way to trade their goods. Onwards – and eastwards – the people spread, until the entire continent was populated. When the Ice Age ended, the land bridge disappeared under the rising seas, and the Native Americans were on their own.

NORTHWEST: THE SEAFARING WOODWORKERS OF THE PACIFIC NORTHWEST COAST FROM SOUTHERN ALASKA TO NORTHERN CALIFORNIA

OVER A MILLION PEOPLE LIVED IN NORTH AMERICA BY 1500

Culture clubs

From the start, each Native American tribe developed its own survival skills and ways of life. This is not surprising considering the differences in geography, climate, and resources found across the continent. They became specialists – mound builders, fishermen, farmers, hunters, cliff dwellers, raiders, weavers, potters, and woodworkers.

Those who lived in similar environments held much in common. This is why anthropologists (people who study human cultures) have divided the North American tribes into 10 culture areas.

PLATEAU: THE ROAMING PEOPLES OF BRITISH COLUMBIA AND THE NORTHWEST

GREAT BASIN: THE HARDY SURVIVORS OF NEVADA AND UTAH

CALIFORNIA: THE HUNTER-GATHERERS OF THE WEST COAST, FROM NORTHERN CALIFORNIA TO BAJA MEXICO

SOUTHWEST: THE DESERT DWELLERS OF ARIZONA, NEW MEXICO, AND NORTHERN MEXICO

LOG ON...
www.nps.gov/bela
Bering Land Bridge home page

WEIRD WORLD
THE ONLY DOMESTIC ANIMALS TO MAKE THE CONTINENTAL CROSSING WITH THE FIRST AMERICANS WERE DOGS. THEY MAY HAVE SERVED AS VALUED HUNTING COMPANIONS... OR DINNER, AT A PINCH.

ARCTIC: THE FROZEN LANDS OF THE INUIT, FROM SIBERIA EAST TO GREENLAND

SUBARCTIC: THE NOMADIC HUNTERS OF ALASKA AND NORTHERN CANADA

NORTHEAST: THE WOODLAND HUNTERS OF NEW ENGLAND, THE MID-ATLANTIC, AND THE GREAT LAKES REGION

PLAINS: THE BUFFALO HUNTERS WEST OF THE MISSISSIPPI RIVER TO THE ROCKY MOUNTAINS, FROM CANADA TO MEXICO

SOUTHEAST: THE VILLAGE FARMERS OF FLORIDA AND THE DEEP SOUTH

13

SPIRIT WORLD

Invisible yet invincible – this is the sacred power of the spirit world at the heart of most Native American religions. There is no single religion among Native Americans, and few tribes believe that one "Great Spirit" is at the controls. But most belief systems share a strong link with the spirit world, and an understanding of its power to influence people's lives. Most Native Americans are sure that everything in nature holds this power, so they try to live in harmony with the Earth.

Spirit power

People depended on spirit power to help them in all kinds of ways – to heal them, protect them in battle, or ensure a successful hunt or a good harvest. Many tribes saw a strong spirit power in things that were important to their survival. For example, there were rain spirits in the desert, and buffalo spirits on the Great

PEOPLE, PLACES, PLANTS, OBJECTS, AND ANIMALS HAD SPIRIT POWER

Plains. Spirits were not always good, and naughty spirits had to be pleased. Whether they were good or not, spirits were reached through special ceremonies or by special people.

A BLACKFEET SACRED THUNDER MEDICINE PIPE IS OFFERED TO THE THUNDER SPIRIT WITH THE FIRST SPRING STORM.

Vision thing

So how did you call up the spirit world? One way was through your own personal guardian spirit. Most tribes believed that everyone had one or more guardian spirits to help them in life. Your spirit first appeared to you in your early teens, in an initiation ceremony known as a vision quest. You set off on your own, away from the madding tribe, and went without food or sleep – sometimes wounding yourself – until you saw a vision of your guardian spirit.

Sacred ceremonies

Another way to get in touch with the spirit world was through special ceremonies. While you might attend a church, synagogue, or mosque, Native Americans gathered in their own sacred places to perform these ceremonies. The ceremonies, steeped in ritual and tradition, were usually led by a priest. Some were held only at certain times of the year (such as harvest time or a new moon), while others marked big events in a person's life (for

PLAINS SHAMANS (SPIRITUAL LEADER AND HEALER) OFFER THANKS AND PRAYERS TO THE SPIRIT WORLD.

CAYUGA FALSE FACE MASK, WORN IN A MYSTERIOUS HEALING CEREMONY FOR AILMENTS SUCH AS HEADACHES.

Meet the shamans

The ultimate link to the spirit world was through a special man or woman we know as a shaman (although each tribe had their own name for these experts). The name comes from an ancient word for "he who knows", and many shaman were deep thinkers, respected by the tribe for their wisdom and their understanding of their faith.

A shaman's job included interpreting dreams, tending to the injured, explaining and expanding tribal beliefs, and healing the sick with a bit of magic and a bit of medicine (which is why the Europeans called them "medicine men" or women). Some of a shaman's cures were a kind of magic. For example, a shaman might suck on a patient's body, then expel the object that had "caused" the illness – a small stick or pebble the shaman had hidden in his or her mouth. But many of the shaman's herbal cures were fantastic remedies, and are still used today.

example, an initiation into a sacred society). There were also ceremonies to renew links with the spirit world, and to pray for things the people needed to survive. Music was a big part of most ceremonies, as tribespeople sang and danced to the rhythmic beat of pebble-filled rattles, wooden clappers, and animal-skin drums.

Medicine pouch

A shaman's healing secrets were carried in a medicine pouch. The most important thing in a shaman's pouch of herbs and remedies was tobacco, thought to have magical powers (it was also used in sacred ceremonies). A shaman often blew a bit of tobacco smoke over a sick person to begin the healing process, and tobacco juice was squeezed onto a snake bite or bee sting to numb the pain.

Shamans in the Southeast treated aches and pains with salicylic acid – better known to us as aspirin. Caffeine, quinine, and herbal teas were also effective healing tools.

LOG ON...
www.nativeamerican
healing.com

Keeping the faith

Although many Europeans who came to the New World were escaping religious intolerance, they were intolerant of the Native American beliefs they encountered. The new arrivals often tried to convert the tribes to Christianity, going so far as to take over sacred sites and outlawing many religious practices. Despite these massive obstacles, many Native Americans managed to keep their traditional beliefs alive.

BEFORE MANY SACRED CEREMONIES, PEOPLE PURIFIED THEMSELVES BY SWEATING OUT BAD SPIRITS IN A SAUNA-LIKE LODGE.

17

MEET THE FAMILY

Pawnee or Pomo, Shawnee or Sioux, Native Americans valued their families. Men, women, and children often had separate roles, but everyone worked together to provide the basics of day-to-day life – food, clothing, and shelter. Relatives lived close to each other (sometimes in the same house), and aunts, uncles, and grandparents helped raise the children and teach them about tribal ways. Families often gathered in the quieter times to catch up and celebrate together.

FAMILY TIES WERE TIGHT AMONG THE TRIBES OF NATIVE AMERICA

Toys and tales

What would your life be like as a Native American child? First of all, you could chuck your schoolbooks. Kids learned what they needed to know by helping their parents and older siblings with their daily chores. Children too small to help were kept close by, as there was a lot to learn simply by watching. They also learned by listening, as their older relatives, especially grandparents, passed on the legends and lore of the tribe (as well as handy household and hunting

AN ARAPAHO CHILD ONCE TREASURED THIS TINY TOY HORSE WITH BLANKET AND REINS.

APACHE CHIEF ANTONIO MARIA POSES FOR A PHOTOGRAPH WITH HIS FAMILY IN 1897. THEY ARE ALL DRESSED IN TRIBAL FINERY.

BOYS PRACTISE THEIR HUNTING SKILLS
WITH HALF-SIZED BOWS AND ARROWS.

hints). But just like you, they also learned by playing. There were all kinds of toys for make-believe, such as tiny bows and arrows, miniature cooking pots, small dolls, and kid-sized tepees. There were loads of games to play, either on your own or in a big competition with a pile of mates. Native people who kept horses had their first riding lessons as soon as they could hang on, and those who lived near water went swimming every day, even in winter.

Testing, testing

Once boys and girls reached their early teens, they probably felt well prepared for their adult roles, as teenagers always seem to know everything. Many tribes held special ceremonies to mark this passage. Some girls were tested to ensure they had learned the

ways of a woman's work day, while boys were evaluated for their bravery and strength. In some tribes, boys were deliberately placed in difficult situations – perhaps left without food in the wilderness

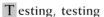

WEIRD WORLD
WOULD YOU WEAR A ROACH, OR JUST STEP ON IT? ROACHES WEREN'T BUGS, BUT LONG STRIPS OF STIFF ANIMAL HAIR, USUALLY DYED RED, TIED TO THE HEAD OF AN EASTERN WARRIOR.

LOG ON...
www.cyndislist.com/
native.htm

to test psychological as well as physical strength. And you thought GCSEs were tough. For both boys and girls, something far more terrifying was just around the corner – finding a partner.

L et's get hitched

Most Native Americans married in their mid-teens. Usually, family members choose partners for their children, but boys had some say in finding their future wives. Once the approach – perhaps a small gift, a love song, or a heavy hint dropped by a female relative –

was made, and if the feeling was mutual, the potential bride and groom tried to win over their future in-laws. A girl might grind corn or weave a basket right outside her boyfriend's house, so his mother could admire her work. Meanwhile her intended was over at her place showering her family with gifts. This was because marriage was not just

AN OJIBWA FAMILY AT WORK AND PLAY AMONG THE BIRCHBARK WIGWAMS OF THEIR GREAT LAKES SUMMER HOME.

TRIBE MEMBERS GATHER INSIDE A MANDAN CHIEF'S LODGE.

between two people, but two families. Once all parties were satisfied, the couple was considered hitched.

Mr and Mrs

Newlyweds tended to move in with the wife's family, sometimes in the same dwelling, but always close by. The young husband was expected to join the family firm – or farm – and to treat his mother-in-law with great respect. In most cases, his job was to provide food, either by hunting or farming. Of course, he still had ties to his own family, but his future children would become part of his wife's family. The new wife carried on with her usual daily tasks, which could include farming, gathering edibles, cooking, making clothes, and looking after the house. Sometimes a young couple moved out when their first child arrived, but often they stayed put, as their relatives were keen to help them raise the children.

Tight ties

Family ties were – and still are – tight in Native America. This was important, especially in more barren areas, because everyone needed to work together to ensure the survival of the family. It was common for extended families – brothers, sisters, uncles, aunts, cousins, grandparents – to live together, sharing the daily work. Of course, those who were frail were only expected to do what they could. Sometimes the extended family was extended even further, to include distant relatives. These groups were known as clans.

Home sweet home

Whether your family was extended or simply exhausted, you needed a place to sleep.

MODEL OF AN EIGHT-FAMILY IROQUOIS LONGHOUSE WITH A WOODEN FRAME COVERED IN ELM BARK.

IROQUOIS HARVESTING BASKET LOADED
WITH DRIED CORN COBS.

The kind of shelter a Native American lived in depended on available materials, local weather, and how long the house was meant to last.

Hunter-gatherers lived in simple shelters that were quick to put up and take down. Most of these were tent-like dwellings, with a framework of wooden poles covered in brush, woven reed mats, or animal hides. Igloos were also pretty quick to assemble.

Farmers, and others who tended to stay in one place, built larger, longer-lasting homes from wooden logs or planks, mud and earth, or stone. Some dwellings could only fit one family, while others housed entire villages. Native Americans made their own home furnishings. Some people were too busy hunting and gathering to bother with comforts, others made their homes cosy.

What's cooking?

The heart of a house is said to be the kitchen, which sounds about right for a typical Native American home. This is because the cooking fire kept everyone warm while dinner was on the boil. The contents of the cooking pot (or box or basket) varied depending on where the tribe lived. Some people ate mostly meat or fish, while others lived on corn, beans, and squash with a little meat thrown in where available. Most Native Americans were expert at finding wild foods, such as roots and berries, to round off their meals.

Food was sometimes cooked outdoors, over a fire or in an oven-like pit lined with stones. Meat and vegetables were often dried and preserved to see people through the leaner times.

SAUK CHIEF KEOKUK WEARS A
FEATHERED HEADDRESS AND
A BEAR-CLAW NECKLACE.

Dressing up

You've slept, you've eaten... but what will you wear? Native Americans wore all kinds of clothes, depending on the weather and what materials were to hand. Most tribes created elaborate clothing for pow-wows, festivals and other special occasions.

For everyday, buckskin, or tanned deer hide, was a wardrobe staple, as were other animal furs and feathers. Tree bark and other plant materials were woven into capes, hats, and sandals. As the temperature dropped, people piled on layers of clothing, since they were busy outside for a large part of the day. Hair was styled with the aid of bear grease or fish oil, and body painting was common for war and special ceremonies.

25

DAILY LIFE

What did people do all day? Hunt, fish, gather, farm, barter, play, and sleep… then get up and do it all over again. There was rarely a dull moment in Native America of the past. A big chunk of each day was spent finding food, but there was also time to tidy the tepee and knock around with friends before hanging up your moccasins for the night.

Happy hunting grounds
Ever since the first Native Americans crossed the frozen land bridge, cold… er, hot on the trail of the woolly mammoth, hunting has been a crucial part of daily life. Even people who grew most of their own food did a little hunting. The most popular targets were fuzzy (deer, bear, buffalo, elk, moose, beavers, and rabbits),

WHAT LIES BENEATH? A FISHERMAN IN HIS CANOE SCANS THE RIVER WATERS FOR FISH AND OTHER SWIMMING SNACKS.

feathery (ducks and geese), and flipper-y (seals, sea lions, and whales). Animals were hunted with the same sorts of weapons tribes took to war, such as clubs, spears, and bows and arrows. In the Southeast, blowguns were used to kill birds and small prey. But none of these weapons were exactly long-range. Hunters had to think strategy – perhaps creeping up on their prey silently, driving the animal into some sort of trap, or stunning it into eventual submission. Many tribes had their own special hunting grounds, which they returned to year after year.

TRIBAL SURVIVAL DEPENDED ON A GOOD SOURCE OF FOOD

Hook, line, and sinker

Tribes who lived near the water were into food that had fins. Spears, harpoons, woven traps and nets, hooks and lines, and bare hands were all used to catch fish. Clams, mussels, eels, and turtles also went into the

HUNTERS ON HORSEBACK AIM ARROWS AT A HERD OF STAMPEDING BUFFALO, VALUED FOR BOTH MEAT AND HIDE.

fishing basket. Many tribes liked to fish at night. The flaming torches on their canoes would attract fish to the surface, where they were easily speared or netted. One of the most sought-after fish in the northern regions was the oily eulachon, or candlefish. Its oil was prized as an all-purpose condiment (seasoning), but the

27

WOMEN PREPARING GATHERED WILD FOODS.

candlefish could also be dried and burned, just like a torch, to light up the night sky (although you might want to hold your nose).

Growing crops

If you can't imagine fish without chips, don't despair – potatoes were one of the crops that were grown on Native American farms (as were tomatoes, peppers, melons, sweet potatoes, and peanuts). But without a doubt, the top three crops were corn, beans, and squash. These crops were easy to grow – in fact, they were often grown together –, tasty and nutritious to eat, and simple to dry and store.

In some tribes men did the farming, while in others women were in charge of the fieldwork. It was tough work – the only tools were wooden digging sticks and stone or bone hoes, and everything was harvested by hand.

One crop almost everyone grew, even the buffalo hunters of the Great Plains, was tobacco, which was part of nearly all special ceremonies.

Gathering a meal

There were plenty of things to eat that were simply there for the taking – berries, nuts, roots, bulbs, seeds, and grains. In fact, some tribes dined almost exclusively on what they were able to gather during the day. For those who lived in dry areas and fancied a drink with dinner, there was even water to gather, stored in the roots of desert plants.

People who gathered food knew that each food had its own season and its place. By following nature's cycles, they were able to find enough food to keep them roaming onwards.

WEIRD WORLD
EXPERTS GUESS THAT MORE THAN HALF OF THE FOODS EATEN ALL OVER THE WORLD TODAY WERE FIRST DOMESTICATED BY THE NATIVE AMERICANS.

SOUTHWESTERN FARMERS DEVELOPED A TYPE OF MAIZE (CORN) THAT COULD THRIVE IN THE DESERT HEAT.

THE WHOLE TRIBE TURNS OUT FOR A GAME OF LACROSSE, A STICK-AND-BALL GAME POPULAR ALL OVER NATIVE AMERICA.

Homework

Once you've hunted, fished, or gathered, dinner is organized, but the day's work is far from done. Maybe your tepee has a hole in it and is starting to leak, the handle's come off your favourite cooking pot, or you've worn out your moccasins. Hour upon hour was spent making and maintaining tools, weapons, clothes, and household goods, as well as looking after the house

TWO STICKS USED IN A CREE THROWING GAME, AND AN ARAPAHO HIDE BALL FOR PLAYING THE PLAINS GAME OF SHINNY.

itself. You couldn't just send things off to the repair shop – most families were expected to take care of things themselves.

Playtime

All work and no play is no fun at all. The Native Americans were mad on games. There were team ball games like stickball and shinny, competitive games such as foot races and hoop-and-pole games, and games of chance. A friendly wager on the outcome was quite common – some Plains people were known to bet their horses and shirts. You wouldn't find men and women

30

Let's move

How did Native Americans get from A to B? Before horses, cattle, and other beasts of burden were introduced, the choice pretty much boiled down to boat or boot (or moccasin or snowshoe). Tribespeople built all sorts of boats, from lightweight one-person canoes to sea-going crafts that packed in a few dozen passengers. There were even furry boats covered in buffalo hide.

People on the move often carried their belongings in backpack-like tumplines. When there was too much to cart about, they hitched a dog to an A-frame carrier called a travois and loaded it up (horses later replaced dogs, who couldn't carry much). In snowy places, flat sleds called toboggans were packed up and pulled along.

on the same team – they played separately, and enjoyed different games. Children often played simplified and scaled-down versions of the grown-ups games.

MODEL OF A MANDAN BULLBOAT, A ONE-PERSON CRAFT MADE OF BUFFALO HIDE STRETCHED OVER A WILLOW FRAME.

Swap shop

If you take a trip across America, chances are part of your journey will be on a route carved out by Native American traders. Early entrepreneurs traded with the tribes next door, and before long a web of trading trails covered the continent. Trading was a brilliant way to get goods that weren't available locally. It also brought tribes together to swap ideas and stories and exchange news. No notes or coins changed hands, although some tribes used objects such as seashells in the same way as money.

Tribes also traded with the Europeans, exchanging animal pelts, hides, and handcrafted goods for metal tools and cookware, guns, horses, and hootch (alcoholic drink). But the more the natives depended on goods made by others, the sooner they lost the skills that had kept them independent.

Talking it over

So how do you make a deal with someone from another tribe, speaking an entirely different language? Though many of the 500 languages spoken in Native America had common roots that might have made a basic conversation possible, the rest probably sounded like gibberish to outsiders. People sometimes got around this by adopting a common trade language, but more often they used gestures

A EUROPEAN TRADER SHOWS CLOTH AND METAL TOOLS TO TWO NATIVE AMERICANS.

SEQUOYAH HOLDS THE CHEROKEE WRITING SYSTEM THAT BROUGHT LITERACY TO HIS PEOPLE.

LOG ON...
www.mcn.net/~wleman/langlinks.htm

to communicate. The Plains tribes developed a system of sign language that enabled them to "speak" with each other.

Write up

For centuries, there was no real written language in Native America. Instead, tribes recorded stories and events with pictures etched into bark or drawn onto animal skins. These pictures didn't quite speak a thousand words, but they certainly helped to jog the memory.

In the 1800s a Cherokee farmer named Sequoyah developed a written language with 86 symbols that stood for syllables in his native tongue. The Cherokees quickly adopted this writing system and soon they were able to write down their laws and legends and keep trading records. Sequoyah's system was also adapted for other tribes to use.

33

WAR CRIES AND PEACE PIPES

No president, no prime minister, not even a head chief... just who was in charge in Native America? The people had the power to make decisions, set rules, solve problems, and settle disputes. Sometimes there was no way to work things out, and hostilities broke out between tribes or individuals. But for the most part they lived peacefully. After the Europeans moved in, it was a different story. Giving in to European demands meant loss of tribal lands, but resistance led to war – and a massive loss of lives.

Hail to the chiefs

The Native Americans organized themselves into bands and tribes. A band might consist of a few families, or the whole family tree. Tribes were much larger than bands, with people living in the same neighbourhood, speaking the same language, and sharing the same customs and beliefs. Both bands and tribes had one or more leaders, sometimes known as chiefs. Often there were different chiefs for different tasks – for example, a peace chief supervised daily life while

THIS SACRED MENOMINEE CALUMET, ADORNED WITH EAGLE FEATHERS, WAS SMOKED TO MARK THE END OF FIGHTING.

a war chief planned battle tactics. Some chiefs inherited the job, but most had to earn the respect of their people – and keep it.

34

Passing the peace pipe
Chiefs shared their authority with other tribal leaders, who were respected by the tribe for their superior ideas and skills. When a problem arose, the property. The war chief shared his plan of attack with the warriors – they had to approach like foxes, fight like lions, and disappear like birds. Once they encountered the enemy –

THE PEOPLE HELD THE POWER IN TIMES OF WAR AND PEACE

leaders gathered together to find a solution. After offering prayers and blowing smoke to the sky, they passed the calumet (an elaborately decorated tobacco pipe) around the circle. Smoking the peace pipe was believed to bring purity and truth to the leaders as they made important decisions.

Warriors
If a council was unable to make a decision, they might declare war. Wars were fought for revenge, to obtain honour, or sometimes to raid another tribe's horses or

A HIDATSA WARRIOR PREPARED HIMSELF FOR BATTLE – OR CELEBRATED VICTORY – WITH DANCE.

hopefully taking them by surprise – they attacked quickly and made a fast getaway, sometimes taking a few captives back home. Particularly skillful moves on the battlefield earned the warrior great honour, a feather or two, and the right to brag about his success.

Weapons of war

Native American warriors battled each other with bows and arrows, lances, spears, and fearsome war clubs carved from wood. You wouldn't want to be on the receiving end of a war club. Some had a grapefruit-sized stone ball at one end to deliver a knockout blow. Others featured axe-like blades and deadly spikes made from sharpened animal antlers. Warriors carved a notch in the club handle for each kill. Among some tribes, collecting the scalp of an enemy brought great honour, but this practice was not particularly widespread.

A larger threat

Everything changed once the Europeans arrived. Early encounters were often peaceful, perhaps because the Europeans

A WARRIOR'S DAKOTA HIDE QUIVER (ARROW HOLDER) AND BOW CASE, WITH BEADED SHOULDER STRAP.

were depending on Native Americans to show them the ways of the (new) world. But it all went up in smoke, and we're not talking about peace pipes. The Europeans wanted Native American lands, as well as their labour, their goods – and their souls – and they used terror and force to get them. European weapons were formidable – not only guns, but also smallpox, influenza, and other diseases the natives hadn't encountered before. As their numbers were diminished by sickness and war, the Native Americans found themselves facing some pretty stark choices.

T ough choices

One choice was resistance to the European takeover. Many tribes bravely followed this path but, with few exceptions, it was a dead end road. Another choice was compliance (giving in under pressure). The government set aside reservations, sometimes hundreds of kilometres away from their original homes, where Native Americans were meant to live apart from whites. Although some tribes submitted to reservation life, many had doubts about giving up their homelands. Perhaps the strongest choice was to compromise with the government by negotiating treaties to establish new tribal lands. But the tribes soon found that promises made in treaties are made to be broken.

LOG ON...
www.yale.edu/lawweb/
avalon/avalon.htm

BATTLES BETWEEN GOVERNMENT TROOPS AND TRIBES WERE BLOODY, BRUTAL, AND DEVASTATING TO NATIVE AMERICANS.

ARTS AND CRAFTS

Native Americans are a crafty bunch, turning the natural beauty all around them – wood, sand, shells, clay, quills, and plants – into naturally beautiful arts and crafts. Many are everyday objects, but that doesn't stop them from being extraordinary to look at. Historically, women created much of the art, often working together in groups. Because tribes traded their finest creations with each other, a woman's skills benefited the whole family.

Wicker wonders

Almost all Native American tribes made (and still make) baskets, using them as carrier bags, cupboards, and cooking pots. Baskets were lightweight, and

A WOMAN MAKES A BASKET FOLLOWING TRADITIONAL TRIBAL TECHNIQUES.

could take a little bashing about without breaking. They could also be made in all shapes and sizes. There were storage baskets, so big that the basket maker had to hop inside to finish them off, bottle-shaped baskets for carrying water, and flat basketry trays to hold the evening meal.

Baskets were made from plant and tree fibres. Some were plaited or woven, while others were made of coiled fibre ropes sewn into place. Sometimes basket makers wove in fibres coloured with natural dyes to make brilliant designs. Other baskets were painted, or decorated with feathers or seashells. Native Americans also used basketry techniques to weave

FINELY ETCHED DESIGNS ENCIRCLE THIS TWO-HANDLED CATAWBA POT.

hats, ceremonial masks, shoes, clothing, mats for inside and outside the house, and even baskets as fish traps.

Top of the pots

From the earliest times, Native Americans who lived near a good source of clay were keen potters. They worked the clay with their hands and tools they had developed for the task – there were no potter's wheels to help them. Pots were used for cooking, serving food, and storing water. Small grave objects and pipes were also crafted from clay.

WEIRD WORLD
PUEBLO POTTERS INSISTED ON SILENCE AROUND THEIR KILNS, AS THEY BELIEVED LOUD VOICES WOULD ROUSE THE SPIRITS IN THE POTS TO SHATTER THEM.

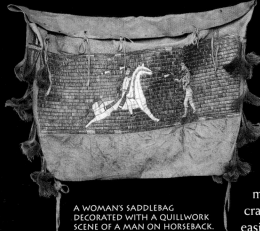

A WOMAN'S SADDLEBAG
DECORATED WITH A QUILLWORK
SCENE OF A MAN ON HORSEBACK.

Finished quillwork had
a raised, shiny surface,
a little like raffia straw.

Brilliant beads

Porcupines must have
been quite relieved
when European traders
arrived with porcelain
and glass beads. Their
brilliant colours were
much admired by native
craftspeople, and it was
easier to make curved lines
with beads than with quills.
Soon intricate beadwork, often
applied in traditional geometric
designs, popped up on
everything from boots to belts.
Strings of beads decorated

Quill decoration

Before beads became available
at trading posts, native peoples
decorated their clothes and
accessories with porcupine

CRAFT SKILLS WERE PASSED FROM GENERATION TO GENERATION

quills. A porcupine has about
30,000 spiky quills in its fur,
and luckily they pop out
quite easily. Once they were
separated from their original
owner, the quills were softened
in water, flattened out, and
coloured with various natural
vegetable dyes. The coloured
quills were sewn onto buckskin
clothing, moccasins, babies'
cradleboards, and pouches to
make beautiful designs.

pottery and children's toys,
and hung from clothing like a
fringe. Beads were also strung
into beautiful necklaces.

Fruits of the loom

Most Native American weaving
was done in the Southwest,
where the Pueblo people had
cultivated cotton. Among the
Hopi people, weaving was a
man's work. Fur, hair, and
feathers were mixed with the

cotton, spun into yarn, and woven on tall looms. These expert weavers shared their skills with the Navajo tribe, who wove amazing patterned blankets from wild mountain goat hair (and later, from sheep's wool) coloured with plant dyes and charcoal.

In the Pacific Northwest, mountain-goat hair was woven with cedar bark to make fabulous ceremonial blankets, while the people of the Southeast created their fashions from the woven bark of the mulberry tree.

A NATIVE AMERICAN'S ART SUPPLIES WERE A CANVAS OF ANIMAL SKIN AND PAINTS GROUND FROM MINERALS IN THE EARTH.

P ainting pictures

Traditionally, Native American artists didn't make paintings to hang on the wall. Instead, painting was used to decorate objects such as birch-bark boxes and buffalo-skin robes. Colours were extracted from berries and bark or made from powdered minerals mixed with water. Hollow rocks or turtle shells made handy paint pots, while sticks, bones, or clumps of hair made good paintbrushes. Hunting and battle scenes were popular subjects, as were geometric designs, animals, and sacred symbols. Many tribes were big on housepainting – some Northwesterners covered their houses with family crests and animals, while Plains tepees were often decorated with a painting of a big moment in the history of the tribe. Pueblo and

WEIRD WORLD

NAVAJO PARENTS RUBBED SPIDER WEBS INTO THE HANDS OF THEIR BABY DAUGHTERS SO THAT THEY WOULD GROW UP TO BE SKILLED WEAVERS.

Navajo sand paintings, made with dry crushed charcoal and stone, were part of an important religious ritual. Later, Native American artists traded with Europeans for pencils, inks, crayons, and ready-made paints.

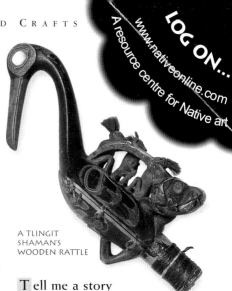

www.nativeonline.com
LOG ON...
A resource centre for Native art

Carved art

The intricate carvings of the Native Americans are twice as impressive when you realize that the carvers also made their own tools. (Iron and steel tools were not available until the Europeans brought them across.) Carving tools were usually made from sharpened shells, animal teeth, and stones. The tribespeople, particularly those in the Northwest, carved hundreds of household objects from wood, as well as elaborate human and animal figures, war clubs, and ceremonial masks. Bone and stone were worked into combs, cutlery, pipes, and other everyday objects. The Inuit even carved snow goggles from ivory, to help shield their eyes from the relentless Arctic glare.

A TLINGIT
SHAMAN'S
WOODEN RATTLE

A HOME-MADE TOOL IS USED TO BORE A HOLE IN TURQUOISE TO MAKE A PIECE OF JEWELLERY.

Tell me a story

Very little Native American literature was written down, and true stories were more often shown as pictures or woven into wampum (strings of seashells). Instead, the native people handed down tribal legends, folk tales, creation stories, and poetry, by word of mouth. Traditionally, it was the role of grandparents to pass along stories to their grandchildren. In recent years, more Native American writers have drawn from these spoken traditions to show how their people experience and explain their world.

43

PEOPLE OF THE WOODLANDS

From the shores of the Atlantic Ocean, west to the Mississippi River, lived the people of the Northeastern culture. Dense forests once covered much of this land, providing good hunting grounds and a ready supply of lumber. Most people settled near water, as there were plenty of fish and sea creatures to eat. They paddled their canoes across the region's waterways.

MAP SHOWING THE NORTHEASTERN CULTURE AREA

The big league
Most of the tribes of the Northeast spoke a variation of the Algonquian language. But one group of nations, who lived in what is now New York state,

SENECA CHIEF CORNPLANTER WAS A FINE IROQUOIS TREATY MAKER.

LAKE-DOTTED WOODLANDS WERE IDEAL FOR FARMING

were a band apart. They had their own language, a ferocious reputation – and the strongest and most powerful alliance in Native American history. These tribes – Mohawk, Onondaga, Seneca, Oneida, and Cayuga (a sixth, the Tuscarora Nation, joined in 1722) – had quarrelled for centuries but set their differences aside to form the Iroquois League. Each tribe within the league sent male representatives

A GROUP OF NATIVE NORTHEASTERNERS SHARE A MEAL IN FRONT OF THE VILLAGE MEETING PLACE.

(chosen by the tribe's women) to the Great Council to make important decisions. The strength of their alliance and the power of the Iroquois war clubs made them formidable enemies.

T ree houses

The natives of the woodlands were surrounded by building materials – otherwise known as trees. After European contact, some native people built snug log cabins, but before that time, most lived in villages made up of domed houses called wigwams. These clever dwellings were quick to put up and take down, and adaptable for all kinds of weather.

Wigwams were made from a framework of arched poles, lashed together with strips of bark. The frame was covered with reed mats, or sewn-together bark strips. In winter, the mats were piled on in layers, then topped with fir branches or leaves for extra insulation.

Iroquois families lived together in bark-covered longhouses. Inside, bark partitions ran along both sides, separating each family's bunk

and storage space from the next door neighbour's place. A line of shared cooking fires ran down the centre aisle, making it quite smoky at times. Up to 20 families (related through the women) shared the longhouse.

Wooden wonders

Of course, wood was not just for wigwams. From snowshoes to storage boxes, trees provided

the raw materials for hundreds of essential items. Mats and carrier bags were woven from bark, while tree roots or bark strips were rolled into strong string. A tree burl could be made into a food bowl. Spoons, ladles, serving trays – even cooking pots with lids – were also made from bark and wood.

Hunters used wood to make bows and arrows, fishing spears, and animal traps, and set sticks along their trails to send messages to others. The most famous wooden wonder was the birch-bark canoe. This handsome craft could be carried by one man, yet was tough enough to take 20 men.

Succotash supper

Tribespeople usually ate one big meal a day, supplemented with snacks of nuts, berries, and

CANOES CARRIED PEOPLE ON FISHING AND TRADING TRIPS, AND TO VISIT RELATIVES.

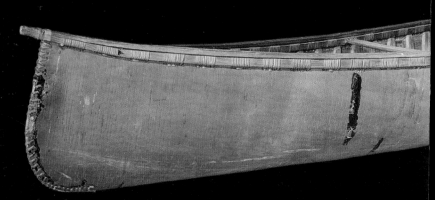

dried meat. Men hunted deer, bear, and moose, or set off in their canoes to fish for eels, salmon, and other finned food, while women paddled along freshwater shores to gather the grain known as wild rice. Meat and fish were either barbecued over an open fire, boiled, or slowly smoked. Most tribes also planted gardens. Corn, beans, and squash, called the "three sisters" by the Iroquois, were grown together in the same patch and often cooked in the same pot (you might know this concoction as succotash). Women pounded corn kernels into a meal that was shaped into cakes and cooked in the ashes of the fire. Leftovers were dried and stored for later.

Tanning deer

Deer was a diet staple, but the outsides of the animal were important too. Each village had

> ### WEIRD WORLD
> SOME NATIVE NORTHEASTERNERS FRIED FOOD ON FLAT STONES PLACED IN THE FIRE, WITH A GENEROUS SMEAR OF RACCOON FAT ON TOP.

a "tanning salon" run by the women. A fresh deer hide was scraped with a tool made from another deer's shinbone to take off the flesh. A good soak and more scraping got rid of the hair. Then, the hide was rubbed with stewed, dried animal brains to soften it, twisted round a tree to wring it out, and finally scraped again.

Skin clothes

What once covered a deer finally ended up covering the tribespeople. Women usually wore belted skirts or

THE CEDAR RIBS OF A BIRCH-BARK CANOE WERE COVERED WITH BIG SHEETS OF BARK LACED TOGETHER WITH SPRUCE ROOTS AND WATERPROOFED WITH SPRUCE RESIN.

simple dresses, topped with a poncho in cold weather. Algonquian men wore a breechcloth or leggings. Iroquois men wore similar clothes but special occasions called for a deerskin kilt. Everyone wore moccasins on their feet, stuffing them with deer hair in the winter to make them warmer. It took an entire deerskin to make around ten pairs of men's moccasins.

Wampum

Strings of white or purple beads made from clam and whelk shells, called wampum, were used by the Northeasterners to record tribal legends and laws, mark special events, or make treaties official. The beads were often woven

THIS PENOBSCOT BUCKSKIN JACKET WITH GLASS-BEADED EMBROIDERY SHOWS THE INFLUENCE OF EUROPEAN MATERIALS.

LOG ON...
www.nativetech.
org/scenes/

FROM 1497 ONWARDS, A STREAM OF EUROPEANS CAME INTO CONTACT WITH THE PEOPLE OF THE NORTHEAST.

into long belts, to tell long stories. Wampum was highly prized and often traded by the native peoples, but it had no fixed value. Once the Europeans discovered its importance to the tribes, they made fake wampum from glass, priced it per string, and used it to trade with the natives.

The first Thanksgiving

The people of the woodlands were among the very first Americans to meet the

OJIBWA TROUGH, LADLE, AND SKIMMER FOR WORKING BOILED MAPLE TREE SAP INTO SUGAR.

Europeans. You can imagine their confusion and surprise. One tribal story from this time describes a tree-covered island sliding towards the shore, with bears crawling over it. In fact the island was a sailing ship, the trees its masts and riggings, and the bears were crew members eager to catch a glimpse of the new land. At first, natives got on fairly well with their new neighbours. In 1621 they even shared their harvest (and farming tips) with the settlers at the first Thanksgiving. But the good relations vanished faster than the turkey leftovers, with the natives not only drawn into small squabbles but also full-on war, as the Europeans fought for possession of the new world. The tribes lost – or struggled to hold on to – their homelands.

PEOPLE OF THE SOUTHEAST

You sleep in a chickee, your favourite game is chunkey, and it's sofkee (also known as grits) again for tea. Whether Creek, Seminole, Chicksaw, Choctaw, or Cherokee, you are proud to live in the lush and fertile Southeast. It's easy to see why – with mild winters, long summers, plenty of deer and bears to hunt and rain to make the gardens grow, there's no need to go anywhere else.

MAP SHOWING THE SOUTHEAST REGION

A major pile-up

The first people to make their mark on the region were the ancient Mound Builders, in about AD 1300. And what marks they were – earthworks up to 30.5 m (100 ft) high and 305 m (1,000 ft) long, built one basket of dirt at a time. It probably took 200 years to construct the grandest of these mounds, which served as tombs, monuments, ceremonial grounds, and even as temple foundations.

Settling down

The descendants of the Mound Builders spread throughout the Southeast, from the Great Smoky Mountains to the shores of the Mississippi River and the swamps of Florida. In this bountiful land villages were built to last and might

CREEK ELDERS MET AT THE COUNCIL ROUND HOUSE.

include a square with public buildings – including a men-only sauna – and a plaza. This open space was the setting for dances and ceremonies, and the ancient stick-throwing game called chunkey. Smaller, family dwellings made of reed and bark were dotted around the square. In very hot places, people lived in chickees – thatched huts raised off the ground to keep snakes and other swamp creatures away. The surrounding

CHEROKEE WOMAN MAKING BASKETS AT OCONALUFTEE VILLAGE IN SOUTH CAROLINA.

farmland was worked on by all the tribespeople. Corn was the main crop, but villagers also grew squash, sweet potatoes, and melons. Children, acting as scarecrows, protected seeds and seedlings from scavengers.

Clan organization

Creek villagers were organized into clans, with the Miko (chief) at the top of the heap. He was more powerful than many other Native American chiefs, and more colourful – his face was painted half black and half red, and he wore a fantastic bonnet of tall swan feathers. Priests, storytellers, and holy men, also held important positions within the tribe.

As for the Miko's subjects, children were treated well, but boys had a rougher time. While girls were named for life, boys kept their birth names only until some act of bravery or daring earned them a better one. The pressure to collect a scalp – and win the respect of the village – was so intense that boys sometimes murdered a mate to get one. Once a boy had proved himself he looked for a bride. No ring was necessary – the groom simply left a deer carcass on his intended's

A YUCHI FEATHER FAN USED BY DANCERS DURING THE GREEN CORN FESTIVAL.

doorstep. If the girl cooked and served it up, the marriage was sealed.

Scratch and retch

One of the strangest customs of the Southeastern tribes was the ritual of scratching. While you might kiss or shake hands with someone you know, the custom in the Southeast was to scratch a buddy all over – sometimes with a sharpened fish bone. Before a big hunt, a major battle, or an important ceremony, men got scratched. Naughty kids were sometimes scratched until they bled, so that the evil inside them could escape. Another unusual custom was the ritual gulp of the "black drink", brewed from holly leaves and believed to be a gift from the Great Spirit. It was common to glug a weak cupful (or hollow gourd full) in the morning for a quick pick-me-up. A stronger brew – strong enough to make you vomit – was taken by warriors to cleanse the body and mind before a battle, or to mark a boy's passage into manhood.

SEMINOLE DOLLS IN TYPICAL CLOTHES WORN BY GIRLS AND WOMEN UNTIL THE EARLY 1900S.

Green Corn Festival

The biggest celebration in almost all Southeastern nations is the yearly Green Corn Festival, marking the late-summer ripening of this valued crop. The villagers put their houses in order in every way, tidying up, doing repairs, and settling debts and disputes. There was a bit of scratching and black-drink slurping, then all the village fires were put out. A new fire was started with ears of corn from the fresh harvest, and the feasting and celebrations began.

Move along

Generation after generation, the native peoples of the Southeast saw no reason to leave their settled homelands. But others wanted the land that had shared its bounty for so long. In the 1830s, the surviving tribes were forced to move to reservations in Oklahoma. So many died during the journey, it became known as the Trail of Tears.

ONE-FOURTH OF THE CHEROKEE PEOPLE WHO TRAVELLED THE TRAIL OF TEARS LOST THEIR LIVES ALONG THE WAY.

BUFFALO HUNTERS

The skies seem to stretch forever over the endless prairie, right in the middle of the continent. This was the Great Plains region, once home to some 30 tribes and millions of buffalo – shaggy beasts that provided clothing, food, and shelter for the native people. The first Plains people settled along rivers and streams, where they farmed in between buffalo hunts. After horses came to the Plains, more native people left their permanent homes and hit the trail, following the buffalo as they criss-crossed the sea of grass.

MAP SHOWING THE PLAINS REGION

Where the buffalo roam

Prairie living was tough. From flash floods and wildfires, to brutal winter blizzards with few trees to stop the high winds that rolled across the grassy hills. But there was also beauty and bounty (the latter in the form of the buffalo). Every summer, most Plains people packed up for the prairie, and the buffalo hunt was on. There was plenty of prey – perhaps 100 million buffalo roamed the region – but it took

incredible bravery and skill to trap and kill these beasts. Ancient Plains hunters tried to goad the buffalo into stampeding over the edge of a cliff or into a small enclosure, where a shower of arrows and spears awaited them. Later on, after horses arrived on the Plains, hunters armed with bows and arrows could ride right up alongside their prey.

Uses for a dead buffalo
From hooves to horns, Plains natives seemed to use every part of the buffalo (including the dung, which was burned instead of hard-to-find firewood). The dead beast was skinned and butchered right on the spot. The killer usually took the valuable hide, the hump, and especially the tongue – a Plains delicacy. The rest of the

THE GREAT PLAINS WAY OF LIFE DEPENDED ON THE BUFFALO

meat and internal organs (including the liver) was divided up among the tribe. Meat that wasn't roasted over the buffalo dung fire and eaten was cut into long strips for smoking. Otherwise it was pounded and mixed with berries and fat to make pemmican, a jerky-like food that kept well. Bones were shaped into shields,

A HUNTER ON HORSEBACK COULD GET CLOSE ENOUGH TO THE MOVING TARGET, HERE A BUFFALO, TO SPEAR IT.

55

Even the bladder had its use, as a storage bag for drinking water.

Living in a tepee

The type of dwelling a Plains family chose depended on whether they were roamers or stay-at-homers. Those who followed the hunt preferred the tepee; a cone-shaped tent made of hide. The tripod-like frame was made of about 20 tall poles lashed together – it took about the same number of thick buffalo skins to piece together the tepee cover. Two smoke wings near the tepee top were moved about to control the draft of the cooking fire. Inside the tepee, wood bed-frames filled with grass and covered with hide blankets were set along the walls. Clothes and food were stored in rawhide pouches called parfleches. A lining about as tall as an adult, often painted with stunning geometric designs, was tied all the way around the inside of the tent. It helped keep the inside dry, and gave a family more privacy (at night, the light of the fire cast shadows on unlined tepee walls, making it extremely easy to see what the

A DAKOTA PADDED SADDLE MADE FROM HIDE STUFFED WITH ANIMAL HAIR.

tools, tool handles – even sled runners. Sinew (the tendons connecting muscle to bone) was dried to make tough string, and the tail became a whip. Horns reappeared as spoons and cups, while hooves were boiled up into a sticky glue.

WEIRD WORLD

TANNING BUFFALO HIDES FOR A TEPEE WAS MESSY. TO SOFTEN THE HIDES AND HELP MAKE THEM WATER-RESISTANT, THEY WERE SMEARED WITH MASHED BUFFALO BRAIN AND SMOKED OVER A BUFFALO DUNG FIRE.

A BLACKFEET TEPEE PAINTED WITH GEOMETRIC DESIGNS AND SWIMMING OTTERS

LOG ON...
www.tipie-tepees-teepees.com

neighbours were up to). In cold weather, people stuffed grass between the lining and the outer cover, providing insulation.

Plains natives who stayed longer in one place built earth lodges. These dome-like dwellings, covered in layers of brush and earth, housed a family, its food and belongings, as well as horses and dogs.

B eads and buckskin

Decorated with beautiful beadwork and fabulous fringes, the clothing worn by natives of the Plains was not very plain at all. Men favoured buckskin breechcloths, long leggings, and shirts, while women wore long dresses over leggings. Everyone wore moccasins. At first, Plains women used dyed porcupine quills to decorate clothes, but later they switched to glass beads, sometimes worked in with elk teeth.

Beadwork was heavy going in more ways than one. It took ages to bead a garment – a hole for each stitch had to be poked with a bone awl – and a finished dress yoke might weigh a stone or more.

Tribal rivals

Rivalry between tribes was a way of life. And so was warfare, which helped people to gain status. Bands of warriors, armed with bows and arrows, clubs, and buffalo-hide shields, swept across the prairies, raiding their neighbours for horses – or for revenge. The Dakota people in particular became legendary warriors, much feared by their enemies. A warrior's bravery and cunning earned him (or her, as women fought alongside men) great respect among the tribe. The highest honours were not for scalping or killing, but for counting coups. A coup was earned in several ways, including stealing an enemy's horse in broad daylight, touching an enemy then getting away, or being first to touch a dead enemy's body.

Meeting time

Although the people of the Plains often scattered to follow buffalo or enemies, there were times when the roaming bands joined with others in their tribe. Peace councils met each summer to hear grievances, interpret dreams, and make plans. Council members, chiefs of all the bands, gathered in a

AN ELABORATE HEADDRESS OF EAGLE TAIL FEATHERS TOPPED OFF THE CEREMONIAL DRESS FOR A DAKOTA ELDER OF THE 1800S.

giant tepee to pass the sacred peace pipe and share their wisdom. Plains people also congregated to celebrate the Sun Dance, a religious festival believed to draw power to the community.

The way of the gun

While horses brought new freedom and prosperity to the Plains, another new arrival –

THE US ARMY'S DEFEAT AT LITTLE BIGHORN MADE THE GOVERNMENT EVEN MORE DETERMINED TO CONQUER THE PLAINS.

the gun – marked the beginning of the end. White hunters armed with firearms quickly wiped out the buffalo crucial to the Plains way of life. Before long the US Army mounted armed attacks against the Plains people to clear the prairie for white settlers. The Native Americans fought back fiercely, but each step forward, such as the defeat of General Custer at Little Bighorn, was countered with a terrible step back, such as the loss of 200 Dakota people at Wounded Knee. Many people were confined to reservations far from their prairie homelands.

THE SURVIVORS

MAP SHOWING
THE GREAT
BASIN REGION

I magine being boiling hot and freezing cold in the same day. You spend each waking hour hunting for food to fill your belly, be it roots, rats, or rabbits. As you cross the baked earth, poking under rocks and scrabbling through sagebrush, you can only dream of night and snuggling up in your rabbit-skin robe as the smell of roasting grasshopper scents the air. Oh, for a cool drink, but that means digging up a yucca plant and slurping the water in its roots. Never mind – you are a resourceful native of the Great Basin.

Moving homes

One of the most hostile environments on the continent, the Great Basin was also one of the most isolated. A ring of high mountains, including the mighty Rockies and the Sierra Nevada, surrounded the flat, arid desert below. Basin tribespeople – Ute, Bannock, Paiute, and Shoshone – didn't build permanent villages, as there were few places with enough plants, animals, and water to support them. Instead,

ROAMING TRIBES CARRIED THEIR
BELONGINGS ON A TRAVOIS, A WOODEN
FRAME HITCHED TO A DOG OR HORSE.

they split into small groups, scattered across the Basin, and roamed around in search of food, carrying their belongings with them. The family home, often a cone-shaped shelter of pine poles draped with dried grasses or bark, was split into sections and toted along as well. In winter the people headed back to gather with the other roamers. This was the time for celebrations, weddings, and family reunions.

RATTLESNAKES GAVE A BIT OF BITE TO THE GREAT BASIN DIET.

What's for supper?

Although the search for supper might take most of the day, there was always enough food to survive (and sometimes enough to feast). Anything edible was fair game (and game, such as rabbits and antelopes, was the fairest of them all). Nuts, roots, grasses, and seeds, especially the sweet seed of the pinon tree known as the pine nut, were diet staples, but rats, grasshoppers, snakes, and crickets were also eaten. Those lucky enough to live near rivers fished with

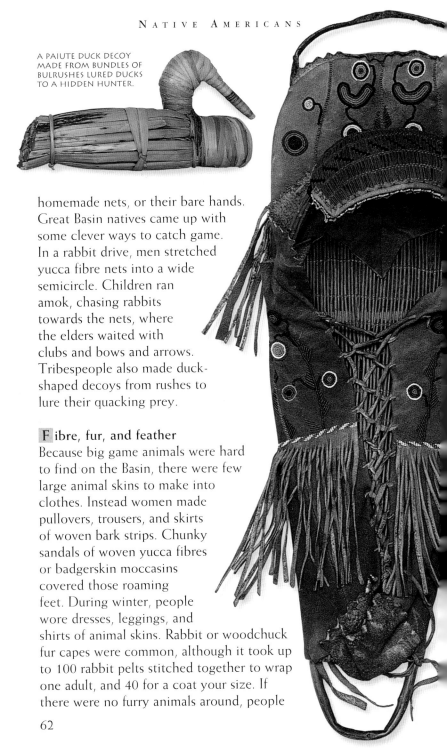

A PAIUTE DUCK DECOY MADE FROM BUNDLES OF BULRUSHES LURED DUCKS TO A HIDDEN HUNTER.

homemade nets, or their bare hands. Great Basin natives came up with some clever ways to catch game. In a rabbit drive, men stretched yucca fibre nets into a wide semicircle. Children ran amok, chasing rabbits towards the nets, where the elders waited with clubs and bows and arrows. Tribespeople also made duck-shaped decoys from rushes to lure their quacking prey.

Fibre, fur, and feather

Because big game animals were hard to find on the Basin, there were few large animal skins to make into clothes. Instead women made pullovers, trousers, and skirts of woven bark strips. Chunky sandals of woven yucca fibres or badgerskin moccasins covered those roaming feet. During winter, people wore dresses, leggings, and shirts of animal skins. Rabbit or woodchuck fur capes were common, although it took up to 100 rabbit pelts stitched together to wrap one adult, and 40 for a coat your size. If there were no furry animals around, people

62

made capes from the feathered skins of several ducks.

P ack it in

People who roam need something to carry their stuff in, so the natives of the Great Basin were great basketmakers. Wide-mouthed baskets were perfect for nut-gathering, bottle-shaped baskets lined with pitch (tar) held drinking water, and pot-shaped baskets were used for cooking

LEARNING THROUGH PLAY: A GIRL HOLDS A TOY CRADLEBOARD FOR HER DOLL.

FOR 10,000 YEARS NATIVE SKILLS SURVIVED IN THE GREAT BASIN

(with a few hot stones from the fire thrown in).

O n horseback

The Basin peoples were among the first Native Americans to use the horse, brought to the region by Spanish explorers. Hunting on horseback was an improvement on roaming, and

BABIES WERE PACKED UP AND CARRIED, TOO – LACED-UP IN A CRADLEBOARD ON MUM'S BACK, SADDLE, OR TRAVOIS.

by the 1700s the horse trade was thriving. Horse ownership became a Basin status symbol.

T rampled in the Gold Rush

The discovery of gold in the Great Basin marked the end of the native people's 10,000-year roam. Fur traders had already begun to nudge the people westward when adventurers and gold miners poured into the region in the 1850s, pushing many people aside for good.

HIGH PLATEAU

MAP SHOWING
THE PLATEAU AREA

The native people of the Plateau lived the high life: snow-capped mountains soared above alpine forests, icy rivers, and sunlit valley floors. There was plenty on the Plateau to eat – fish, big game, and plants – and the mountains provided a natural barrier against enemy attack. Like their close neighbours in the Great Basin region, Plateau people spent spring and summer on the move, hunting and gathering as much food as possible.

Go fish

The tribespeople of the Plateau began stocking up on food each spring. Men bagged rabbits and plucked ducks, while women dug around for roots and seeds. In summer, the rivers filled with salmon, and entire tribes fished, with nets, fish traps, and spears, hoping to catch enough salmon to see them through the year. To snare the salmon swimming upstream to breed, some braver types built log platforms over the rivers. Perched on the ends, they dangled big nets into the water to lift out the catch of the day, which was later dried

THE NEZ PERCE TRIBE PACKED UP THEIR MEALS TO TAKE AWAY IN FLAT BAGS MADE OF TWISTED AND DYED CORNHUSKS.

or smoked. In the autumn, the Plateau women harvested the sweet bulbs of the camass, a relative of the lily, while the men hunted deer, elk, antelope, and bighorn sheep. By October, it was time to head for home, laden with snacks.

Digging in for the winter

The people of the Plateau spent their summers in brush-covered shelters that were easy to pack up and move about. When the chill of winter set in, people returned to their permanent villages to pow-wow and to pray for good

PLATEAU HORSEMAN IN CEREMONIAL DRESS – BEADED AND QUILLED SHIRT AND LEGGINGS, TOPPED WITH A FEATHERED WAR BONNET.

health and good harvests. They bundled up in toasty pit houses, built by digging a big hole in the ground, then putting posts round the edges to make walls. Dirt was piled over the protruding posts to make a cone-shaped roof, with a small hole left at the top for smoke to escape. There was no door – the only way in or out was through the smoke hole. So, friends really did drop in.

PLATEAU HUNTERS HOPED TO BAG BIG GAME LIKE MOOSE (ABOVE) AND BEAR.

Mad hatters

Plateau people were well dressed, as there were so many skins available to fashion into clothing. Men often wore leggings, shirts, and robes of deerskin, mountain goatskin, or sheepskin, while women wore

of the native people of the region. On horseback, they could go further and hunt bigger – even buffalo. Horses

BOYS OF THE THOMPSON TRIBE USED CHILD-SIZED BOWS (WITH UNTIPPED ARROWS) FOR HUNTING PRACTICE.

THE PEOPLE FOLLOWED AGE-OLD TRADITIONS WITH THE SEASONS

dresses. If no skins were handy, clothing was woven from tree bark. The Plateau women also made snug-fitting basket-like hats, woven from leaves, which were not worn anywhere else.

Horse sense

Soon after hoof-beats first sounded on the Plateau in the 1700s, horses changed the lives

also became important status symbols, especially among people used to roaming around on foot. The Nez Perce (or "pierced nose") tribe quickly gained a reputation for horse breeding and trading. Their most famous breed was the Appaloosa, a beautiful spotted horse named after the Palouse River in Oregon.

LOG ON...
Official Nez Perce home page
www.nezperce.com

AN ANTLER SPIKE MADE THIS
WAR CLUB A LETHAL WEAPON .

On expedition

Although the mountains that surrounded the Plateau helped keep the peace for generations, it wasn't long before outsiders arrived. Perhaps the first non-Native Americans to encounter the Plateau natives were Merriwether Lewis and William Clark, who were sent by President Thomas Jefferson to explore the newly acquired western territories of the United States in 1804.

Lewis and Clark enlisted a Shoshone woman named Sacagawea as a guide and interpreter on their famous expedition. Her skills were invaluable, and tribespeople saw her presence as a sign of peace (war parties didn't include women). Soon afterwards, land seekers, fur traders, and miners poured into the Plateau and laid claim to its land, leading to fierce battles. The fight against disease was just as deadly. Half the people were wiped out, and before long the rest were driven from their ancestral homelands.

DESERT DWELLERS

MAP SHOWING THE
SOUTHWEST AREA

Among the spectacular painted deserts, purple mountains, and stark red-rocked canyons lived the native peoples of the Southwest culture area – Apache, Navajo, Pima, Papagao, and Pueblo, or village people. They weren't new in town – their ancestors had put down roots some 2,000 years earlier. Over generations the native peoples learned to cope in, and finally conquer, the desert. The Pueblo in particular established fabulous hilltop villages and fertile fields.

Pueblo influence

The Pueblos were not a single tribe – they included Hopi, Zuni, and Cochiti – and each culture spoke a different language. Their neighbours, the Apache and Navajo, liked what they saw of the Pueblo way of life – so much so that they frequently raided the Pueblos for food and other goods.

A real cliffhanger

Think about the most elaborate sandcastle that you ever created, with tiers, turrets, and tall look-out towers. Imagine that this structure is big enough to house you, your neighbours,

maybe even an entire village. Many Pueblo people lived just like this, in massive, multi-storey dwellings of 200 rooms tucked in the hollows of a

THE TAOS PUEBLO IN NEW MEXICO IS THE OLDEST SURVIVING MULTI-STOREY PUEBLO IN THE UNITED STATES.

mountain, or rising from the flat top of the mesa (high rocky plateau). These tower blocks were built from stones, mesa clay, and wooden beams, to a plan paced out by the village chief. Each family shared a front room, with smaller back rooms for storage. In the oldest dwellings, there were no doors – you came home by climbing a ladder up to the roof, then down another ladder in the smokehole. Later on there were doors,

and even windows filled with light-coloured gypsum rock.

Although living on top of a cliff did offer protection from attack (you could always pull in your ladders if an enemy made the climb), imagine the slog. Building materials had to be hauled up the cliffside, and once people settled in, water and food had to be lugged up

too. Of course, not all Southwesterners lived on top of each other. Navajo families built hogans, log-framed, mud-plastered houses, while Apaches who were done roaming bedded down in brush-and-grass wickiups or tepees.

A YOUNG HOPI GIRL WEARS THE ELABORATELY COILED SQUASH-BLOSSOM HAIRDO.

into two big buns standing out from her head, meant to resemble squash blossoms. Married women wore their hair down, in twin ponytails wrapped to look like squash fruits. Women usually wore one-shoulder dresses woven from cotton and dyed with plant extracts. Her moccasins were not

Going underground

No Pueblo village was complete without one or more kivas, round rooms dug under the ground topped with a wooden roof. These sacred places were like temples, courtrooms, and men-only meeting places in one. A fire altar burned inside, while carvings of animals and spirits decorated the mud-plastered walls. Some kivas had holes in the floor to symbolize the entrance to the underworld. Except on special occasions, only adult males of the village were allowed into the kivas.

Hair and hide

One thing that may have kept a Hopi girl out of the kiva was the size of her hair. An unmarried girl styled her hair

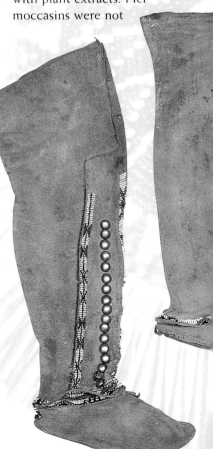

SOFT APACHE BOOTS MADE FROM ANTELOPE OR DEER SKIN WERE PERFECT FOR TRAMPING THROUGH THORNY BRUSH.

LOG ON...
www.indianpueblo.org
Meet the people of the Pueblo

PUEBLO WOMEN SPENT
HOURS EACH DAY
GRINDING CORN KERNELS
AGAINST ROUGH-
TEXTURED STONES TO
MAKE CORNMEAL.

unlike a dancer's legwarmers, with hide strips woven up and around the lower leg. It took a whole deer hide to make a pair of these. Pueblo tribesmen also wore cotton clothing. On special occasions this included a white kilt with a woven sash. Some men wore a headband. The Apache and Navajo dressed mostly in skin clothing, but once the Navajo learned to loom they made cotton clothes.

Amazing maize

The Apache and Navajo were for the most part hunters and gatherers. But over several generations, the Pueblo people worked out how to make even the driest desert bloom with beans, squash, cotton, tobacco, and especially maize, the top crop. The villagers grew more than 20 different types of corn. They planted their fields over underground streams, and worked out ways to divert groundwater towards their crops. While men did most of the farming, women prepared the food. Drying out the corn in the arid desert was easy, but grinding it into cornmeal really was a grind. Corn kernels were rubbed between stones to make the meal, which was tossed into a stewpot for thickening or fried on hot rocks to make tortilla bread.

WEIRD WORLD

HAIR PLAYED AN IMPORTANT ROLE IN HOPI ROMANCE. IF A GIRL COMBED A BOY'S HAIR IN PUBLIC, MARRIAGE WAS ON THE CARDS. AT THE WEDDING, THE GROOM GOT A SHAMPOO FROM HIS MOTHER-IN-LAW TO BE.

Kachina

Quite a few turkey feathers went into the costumes representing the kachinas, or cloud spirits. The Pueblo dwellers believed that the kachinas connected the spirit world with the human world. The spirits dwelled in the mountains, but returned to the village at the same time each year, entering the bodies of masked and costumed tribesmen to lead dances (especially rain-making ones). The spirits used kachina dolls, small effigies carved in their likenesses, to teach children about the spirit world.

HOPI CHILDREN LEARNED ABOUT THEIR RELIGION FROM KACHINA DOLLS. THESE REPRESENT AHOLI AND NAKACHOK.

Calendar sticks

How did the people know when the kachinas would return? They looked at the

calendar stick. The Pueblo people kept an eye on the desert skies, tracking the movements of the sun, moon, and stars. A notch on a calendar stick marked each passing day, sunrise to sunset, and each passing month (which started with the appearance of a crescent moon) was also recorded. Also, the calendar stick helped the people work out the best dates for festivals, planting, and harvesting.

APACHES SUCH AS GERONIMO (FAR RIGHT) FOUGHT HARD TO RESIST THE SPANISH, BUT EVENTUALLY SURRENDERED.

PUEBLO CULTURE THRIVED IN THE DESERT FOR 2,000 YEARS

Pots, blankets, and baskets
Because so few Southwestern tribes were roamers, they made beautiful pottery. Clay cooking pots and storage jars were shaped with tools made of dried-up squash, and painted with yucca-leaf brushes dipped in a mineral and water paste before being fired. Papago and Pima people were best known for their basketry. While they made baskets, the Pueblo made homegrown cotton on the only looms used by Native Americans. They passed their secrets to the Navajo, whose blankets were highly prized.

Spanish imposition
The quest for gold brought Spanish explorers into the Southwest in the 1540s, and Spanish missionaries soon followed. While contact with the Spanish had its rewards – the native people learned new skills such as growing fruits, tending cattle and sheep, crafting jewellery, and making adobe bricks – punishment was brutal as lands were taken and people enslaved. The Pueblo struck back, overthrowing Spanish rule for 20 years before they were eventually overcome once again.

THE WEST COASTERS

Sunny skies, beautiful scenery, and plenty of nuts – this probably sounded like home to the native people of the west-coast California culture area. Many small tribes populated the area between the Great Water (the Pacific Ocean) and the Grandfather Mountains (the Sierras). For the most part, the people lived peacefully, hunting, gathering, and trading. There was plenty of food to go around, and so little need for farming, which meant more time for games, dancing, and ceremonies.

California casual

Because it rarely got cold, the first Californians didn't wear much clothing. Men, if they wore anything at all, favoured animal skin breech-cloths, while women dressed in simple, kilt-like skirts. If it turned cool, people snuggled up in rabbit-fur robes. The style of shelter

A POMO THRESHER WOVEN FROM WILLOW WAS USED TO KNOCK SEEDS INTO A BASKET.

also depended on the local weather. In chillier places, people dug pit houses or built them from wooden planks. Where there was more sunshine, tribespeople lived in cone-shaped thatched huts.

> ### WEIRD WORLD
> NORTHERN CALIFORNIANS WOVE NATIVE RUSH, OR TULE, INTO MATS AND ATTACHED THEM TO FRAMES TO MAKE SHELTERS. TULE MATS LET AIR PASS THROUGH WHILE BLOCKING THE SUN – NATURAL AIR CONDITIONING.

Acorns galore

No doubt each of the 100 languages spoken in California had a word for "acorn", the staple food of the

POMO BURDEN-BASKETS LIKE THIS WERE
USED TO GATHER PLANTS AND THRESHED
SEEDS, TRAP ANIMALS, AND COOK FOOD.

region. Women were in charge of collecting acorns, combing the forest floor for these nutritious, if not exactly delicious, seeds.

The seeds were stored in huge quantities – hundreds of thousands of pounds, enough to turn a squirrel green with envy. Because acorns contain tannic acid (the same stuff that makes tea taste bitter) they had to be carefully treated before eating. They were washed, then ground into coarse meal, which was stuffed into baskets hung over a sandpit. Water was poured into the baskets and drained through. This water removed the tannin as it ran into the sand. Then, the acorn meal was dried and eaten raw, or cooked into a porridge-like

75

NORTHERNERS KEPT THEIR "SEASHELL" MONEY IN PURSES MADE FROM ELK ANTLERS.

NORTHERNERS KEPT THEIR "SEASHELL" MONEY IN PURSES MADE FROM ELK ANTLERS.

mush. The rest of the native Californian diet varied, depending on location.

Coastal tribes ate clams and shellfish, while further inland they hunted game and netted salmon.

Boat builders

The tribes who lived along the Pacific coastline were excellent boat builders. The Chumash

CALIFORNIAN TRIBES LIVED A LAID-BACK LIFE WITH FEW WARS

people made ocean-going canoes called tomols from driftwood collected at the beach. They split the wood into planks, drilled holes along the edges, then sewed the planks together with cord made from milkweed. A layer of tar and pitch made the canoe watertight. Each canoe usually held a crew of two men, as well as a boy to help with the bailing. Whenever a new canoe

was launched, the villagers gathered on the beach to celebrate the occasion.

Tribal traders

Many tribes established strong trading links with others in the region. Acorns were traded for dried fish, baskets exchanged for bows, and seeds swapped for seashells. Some of these seashells were threaded onto strings and used like money.

LOG ON...

For more on California culture

www.ceres.ca.gov/nahc/

The Yurok people used shell strings not only to buy goods and services, but also to pay penalties. For example, the Yuroks "charged" two strings of seashells for a boat, five strings for a plank house, and ten strings for a rich wife (a poor wife was a bargain at just eight strings). Penalties ranged from two strings for speaking a dead man's name to 15 strings for murdering an important person.

On a mission

In 1789 the Spanish government expanded its empire in Mexico, establishing a chain of 21 compounds called missions along the California coast. Spanish missionaries hoped to convert the native peoples to the Catholic faith, and so strengthen Spanish control. Many people came to the missions, providing the huge labour force needed to keep them ticking over. But in return, they got smallpox, measles, flu, and a host of other new diseases that wiped out nearly half the population. Those left standing took another blow when gold was discovered in 1849. Miners hoping to get rich quick poured into the region, pushing aside the original Californians who had enjoyed the region's natural riches for centuries.

A CHUMASH COUPLE OF THE 1880S POSE IN THE FARMYARDS SURROUNDING THE MISSION AT SANTA BARBARA, CALIFORNIA.

TOTEM TRIBES

Water, everywhere water – not just in the rivers and the sea, but also falling from the sky. The rains of the Pacific Northwest fed the growth of huge evergreen forests, and the rivers and sea provided so much food that there was little need for farming. Some 30 tribes lived among the forests and fiords of the Northwest culture region, most settling the narrow stretch of land between the ocean and the coastal mountains.

MAP SHOWING THE NORTHWEST CULTURE REGION

TOTEM POLES TELL THE TALES OF THE PACIFIC NORTHWEST

Animal houses and poles

A typical village consisted of wooden houses – each big enough for one chief and about 40 relatives – made of cedar-log poles covered with split cedar planks. The houses were painted with fantastic designs depicting all sides of an animal, even the insides. In front of the houses stood totem poles, tall cedar columns carved and painted with family legends.

SOME TOTEM POLES WERE USED AS DOORWAYS INTO THE HOUSES, WHILE OTHERS STOOD ALONE.

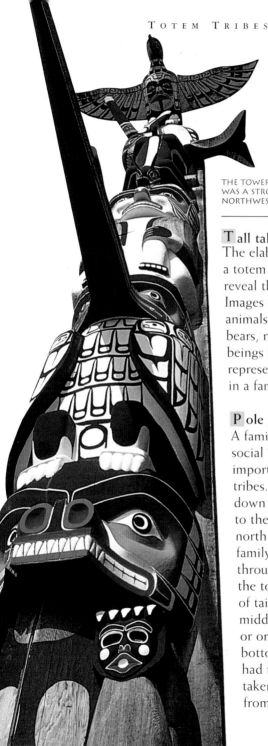

LOG ON...
http://content.lib.
washington.edu/aipnw

THE TOWERING TOTEM POLE
WAS A STRONG SYMBOL OF THE
NORTHWEST TRIBES.

T all tales

The elaborate carvings on
a totem pole are chosen to
reveal the story of a family.
Images of family members,
animals such as thunderbirds,
bears, ravens, and whales, or
beings from the spirit world
represent important events
in a family's history.

P ole position

A family's position on the
social "totem pole" was very
important among Northwest
tribes. Families handed
down their social standing
to their children (in the
north through the mother's
family, and in the south
through the father's). At
the top were the families
of taises, or chiefs. In the
middle were the michimis,
or ordinary people. At the
bottom (for those who
had them) were slaves,
taken in trade or captured
from another village.

79

Bark macs and basket hats

Most tribespeople didn't bother
with clothes or shoes, apart
from the leather pants and tops
worn in the chillier north. The
biggest problem was staying
dry. People wore basketry hats
shaped like big upside-down
bowls. Their poncho-like
"macs" were made from cedar-
bark yarn. When it was time
to dress up, both sexes wore
cedar-bark tunics belted at the
waist, sea-otter fur capes, and
painted hats. They popped in
their finest seashell nose
ornaments (pierced ears and
noses were common) and
sometimes labrets (oval plugs
worn in a hole in the lower lip).

We're going on a whale hunt

Finding food was a doddle in
the Northwest. If you were
tired of fishing around for
something to eat, you could
bag a bear or club a caribou.
There were also berries, bulbs,
and birds' eggs to gather. A
dead whale was a good find,
for its meat, oil, bone, and
sinew. The Nootka didn't wait
for a whale to wash up – they
went to sea in wooden canoes,
armed with harpoons made
from sharpened mussel shells.
After several pokes the whale
was stuck, so crewmen speared
its heart to finish the job before
towing it back.

Secret dances

It wasn't just totem
poles that showed off
woodworking skills.
Some of the most
incredible carving is
found on the wooden
masks worn during
initiations into secret
societies. Two-headed
serpents, eagles that
turned into humans, wild
men, and wolves – masks
and costumes turned dancers
into the characters bound up
in tribal legend. Special
effects included kelp tubes
that made spooky voices in
the rafters and bladders of
seal blood that popped to great
and gory effect. The drums and
the shaman's rattle provided a
hypnotic soundtrack.

A FISHERMAN SPEARS SALMON FROM THE
RIVER, PERCHED ON A ROCKY OVERHANG.

A WOODEN
KWAKIUTL MASK
TRANSFORMS A
BIRD'S FACE INTO
A HUMAN ONE.

Let's potlatch

The important
ceremony among
the totem tribes was the
potlatch. Any special event –
birth, marriage, naming a
chief – called for this feast. A
potlatch lasted for days, with
storytelling, dancing, and food.
The host handed out fantastic
presents to the guests.

Soft gold

By the late 1800s the first
European ships were making
their way up the Pacific coast,
in search of "soft gold", or sea-
otter fur. Many tribespeople
were happy to set up shop, and
were keen to trade for iron
tools. Before long, totem poles
were taller, potlatches
grander, and houses bigger.
Diseases and greedy settlers
threatened the old ways, but
many native people held their
own in their ancient homeland.

A PATTERNED CHIKAT DANCING DRESS IS
WOVEN FROM CEDAR BARK AND DYED
MOUNTAIN GOAT'S HAIR.

THE FROZEN NORTH

MAP SHOWING THE
ARCTIC AND
SUBARCTIC REGIONS

They lived near the top of the world, but the conditions were rock bottom. The winter cold turned the seas into ice, and blizzards brought life to a standstill. Summertime was no picnic either. It was over so quickly that there was no time for farming. Fighting off starvation dominated each ever-shortening day, while mosquitoes that bred in mushy puddles were happy to feast on you. Still, the ingenious natives of the Arctic and Subarctic region survived there for generations. With few raw materials they devised clever ways and special equipment to help them adapt to their chosen home.

Under cover

Northern natives made shelters from whatever was available – even snow and ice. Where there were trees or bits of driftwood, they built wigwams, covering them with bark or animal skins. Roaming tribes lived in pack-up-and-go teepees. Those in the forests built log houses. Some tribes spent the summer in tents, the winter in snow houses.

Inside a snow house

Snow doesn't exactly spring to mind when you think of a good building material for a warm, dry house. But the Inuit igloo gave good protection against the elements because its domed shape trapped rising warm air. The first job for an igloo builder was finding the right

THE IGLOO'S SLOPING ENTRANCE TUNNEL
KEEPS OUT COLD DRAUGHTS.

snow – smooth and firm, and usually from a single drift.

The snow was cut into blocks with a snow knife. Blocks were laid in a neat spiral with a chimney hole at the top, and any gaps were plugged up with softer snow. A window above the entrance was filled with clear ice or a piece of seal intestine.

Inside the igloo was a large snow platform, covered in skins or furs for sitting and sleeping. A lamp that burned seal blubber provided light and heat, and served as a cooker and clothes drier. Some people built separate, small snow-houses to use for storage, dog-houses, and toilets.

WATERPROOF INUIT ANORAK MADE FROM SEAL INTESTINES

The layered look

However cosy your shelter, you had to come out eventually. The natives knew that the key to staying warm is dressing in layers. The first layer was often a caribou-skin shirt and a one-piece garment that combined leggings and "moccasins". Both were worn fur-side in. The next layer was a hooded caribou jacket and thick pants, with tall fur boots filled with a sock-like lining of woven grass or bird skin. A fur cap and mittens gave extra warmth.

Hunting and fishing

Meat and fish were the staple diet in the frozen lands, with a few plants and berries thrown in. Seals were a popular snack in the Arctic, while salmon, caribou, moose, bear, elk, and buffalo were also on the menu in the Subarctic. Meat and fish were either roasted and smoked, stewed, or eaten raw.

From season to season the native peoples followed their prey. Springtime meant piling into seal-skin boats in pursuit of a whale. In summer, there were caribou to hunt and ducks and geese to catch. In winter, hunters crisscrossed the drifts on their snowshoes to hunt down big game. Seals were plucked from icy seas as they came up for air.

Skin trade

The natives of the frozen north managed to hang on to their ways for longer than other culture groups, partly because the region was so isolated. When Russian and European fur traders and whalers pushed their way into the native lands, any previous goodwill melted like an igloo in the desert. The natives traded furs for weapons, but this thinned out the animal stock and soon the people starved. Before long the native people's way of life was changed forever.

AS THE ICE BROKE UP SEALS AND WALRUSES WERE HUNTED FROM ONE-PERSON CANOES CALLED KAYAKS.

REFERENCE SECTION

Whether you've finished reading *Native Americans*, or are turning to this section first, you'll find the information on the next eight pages really helpful. Here are all the facts and figures, background details, and unfamiliar words that will add to your knowledge. You'll also find a list of website addresses – so, whether you want to surf the net or search out facts, these pages should turn you from an enthusiast into an expert.

NATIVE AMERICAN TIMELINE

c.35,000 BC A land bridge is open between Asia and America. Animals roam across it, but there is little evidence of human travel. The bridge eventually disappears.

c.26,000 BC The land bridge opens again. Most experts believe that the earliest Americans were crossing by this time.

c.10,000 BC People were definitely crossing the bridge by now, as ancient tools and evidence of hunting and camping have been found.

c.5000 BC Near the Great Lakes, native people develop the Old Copper Culture, making metal tools.

c.4000 BC The ancient ancestors of the Inuit appear in the far north.

c.300 BC The Hopewell civilization flourishes in river valleys across much of the Midwest and East.

c.900 AD The Moundbuilders (or the Mississippian culture) settle the lands from the Mississippi River east to the Atlantic Ocean.

c.900 The Anasazi build the cliffside community of Pueblo Bonito in New Mexico.

c.1000 The first known encounter between Europeans and Native Americans, between Vikings and Inuit people on Newfoundland.

c.1200 Ancestors of the Apache and Navajo move to the Southwest.

c.1400 The formation of the Iroquois league.

1492 Spanish-backed Italian explorer Christopher Columbus lands in the West Indies. Thinking he is in India, he calls the native people Indians.

c.1500 Thule culture established in the Arctic.

c.1500 The first native North Americans fall to European diseases, which they have no immunity to.

1565 The Spanish found the first permanent European settlement in North America, at St. Augustine in Florida.

1620 Pilgrims arrive from England; the native peoples suffer a huge smallpox epidemic.

1629 The Spanish begin founding missions in the Southwest.

1680 Pueblo tribes stage a successful revolt against Spanish domination.

1689 The first of several colonial skirmishes between France, England, and their Native American allies.

1751 Colonial statesman Benjamin Franklin bases his Albany Plan of Union on the Iroquois League. Its central ideas later appear in the US Constitution.

1754–63 French and Indian War (the colonial phase of the Europe's Seven Years War).

1761 Aleut peoples revolt against Russians in Alaska.

1763 King George III sets aside land west of the Appalachians for the native peoples. The settlers ignore him.

1765 The first reservation is established in Canada.

1787–89 The new US Constitution gives the federal government power to regulate commerce with native tribes.

1803 The Louisiana Purchase opens up lands west of the Mississippi. Plans begin to resettle Eastern tribes there.

1804–06 The Lewis and Clark expedition helps open the West to white settlers.

1809–11 Shawnee chief Tecumseh seeks to unite tribes of the Great Lakes, Southeast, and Ohio Valley against the US.

1809–23 Sequoyah creates his Cherokee alphabet.

1825 The US reservation system begins, with the establishment of a separate Indian Territory west of the Mississippi.

1817 The first of two Seminole wars waged by the US against Florida natives.

1830 The Indian Removal Act leads to a forced removal (1831–39) of Southeastern tribes to Indian Territory further west.

1848–49 As the Gold Rush begins, the tribes in the West are put under pressure by a new wave of settlers.

1851–1869 Indian Wars rage between Native Americans and the US government in the West. Chief Red Cloud leads his warriors to one victory over the US Army, but overall, the Native Americans suffer devastating losses.

1867 US purchases Alaska from Imperial Russia.

1871 Congress confirms its last treaty with Native Americans.

1885 The last great herd of buffalo is exterminated.

c.1900 The population of Native Americans reaches less than 250,000.

1934 US Indian Reorganization Act provides for tribal self-government and landholding.

1946 US policy of termination begins, as the government seeks to end special privileges for tribes.

1951 Canadian Indian Act gives native people the right to vote.

1961 Birth of modern Native American rights movement.

1964 US Civil Rights Act prohibits discrimination by colour, race, religion, or national origin.

1965 Voting Rights Act ensures equal voting rights.

1969 Activists occupy Alcatraz Island in San Francisco, to draw international attention to the plight of native peoples.

1970s–present day Many Native Americans turn to the courts to seek the return of their lands.

1973 A protest at the site of Wounded Knee ends with the death of two Native Americans.

1978 Congress passes the American Indian Freedom of Religion Act, to ensure First Amendment protection for all Native Americans.

1988 Congress passes Indian Gaming Regulatory Act, as some tribes open highly profitable casinos on reservations.

1990 The Native American Graves Protection and Repatriation Act returns to Native Americans the skeletons, stolen grave goods, and other artifacts housed in museums.

2003 Scheduled opening of the National Museum of the American Indian in Washington, D.C.

REGIONAL TRIBAL LIST

Native Americans are proud to identify themselves as members of a tribe. The origins of tribal names are not always easy to trace. Some describe the habitats – or habits – of the people. For example, Hualepai means "people of the tall pines", while Chumash describes "people who make the shell bead money". Other names – not always flattering ones – were given by a neighbouring tribe (Apache is a Zuni word for "enemy"). Some tribe names were acquired from Europeans, and stuck over time, while the origins of others have simply been lost. A list of Native American tribes by region includes:

Northeast tribes
Tribes: Abnaki, Angonquin, Assiniboin, Cayuga, Chippewa, Delaware, Eastern Cree, Eastern Dakota (Santee Dakota, Teton Dakota, Yankton Dakota), Eno, Fox, Honiasont, Huron, Iroquois, Malecite, Massachuset, Mattaponi, Menominee, Micmac, Mohawk, Mohican, Monacan, Moneton, Montagnais, Montauk, Mosopelea, Nanticoke, Narragansett, Nottoway, Oneida, Onondaga, Ottawa, Paleoindian, Pamlico, Pamunkey, Passama-Quoddy, Pennacook, Penobscot, Pequot, Pocomtuc, Potawatomi, Powhatan, Saponi, Seneca, Susquehanna, Tobacco Nation, Tuscarora, Tutelo, Waccamaw, Wampanoag, Winnebago.

Southeast tribes
Ais, Alibamu, Apalachee, Biloxi, Calusa, Catawba, Cheraw, Cherokee, Chickasaw, Chitimacha, Choctaw, Cusabo, Guale, Hitchiti, Houma, Kaskinampo, Koasati, Koroa, Kusso-Natchez, Lower Creeks, Quapaw, Santee, Seminole, Taensa, Taino, Tekesta, Timucua, Tunica, Upper Creeks, Waccamaw, Wateree, Yamasi, Yazoo, Yuchi.

Plains tribes
Tribes: Arapaho, Arikara, Blackfeet, Blood, Caddo, Cheyenne, Coahuilteco, Comanche, Crow, Gros Ventre, Hidasta, Illinois, Iowa, Kanza, Karankawa, Kichai, Kickapoo, Kiowa, Lakota Sioux, Lipan Apache, Mandan, Miami, Missouri, Omaha, Osage, Oto, Paducah Apache, Pawnee, Piegan, Ponca, Quapaw, Rosebud Sioux, Shawnee, Sicangu Lakota, Sutaio, Tawakoni, Tonkawa, Western Kree, Wichita.

Great Basin tribes
Gosiute, Jicarilla, Mono, Paiute, Paviotso, Ute, Washo.

Plateau tribes
Bannock, Bella Coola, Cayuse, Chilcotin, Coeur d'Alene, Flathead, Kalispel, Klamath, Klikitat, Kutenai, Lillooet, Methow, Modoc, Molala, Nez Perce, Okinagan, Pend D'oreilles, Sarsi, Shoshone, Shuswap, Spokan, Thompson, Tunahe, Umatilla, Walla Walla, Yakima.

Southwest tribes
Coyotero Apache, Hopi, Keres, Maricopa, Mescalero Apache, Mimbreno Apache, Mohave, Navajo, Opata, Papago, Pima, Tanoan, Tarahumara, Wallapai, Yavapai Apache, Yuma, Zuni.

Californian tribes
Achomawi, Atsugewi, Cahuilla, Chemehuevi, Chumashan, Cocopas, Costanoan, Diegueno, Gabrieleno, Hupa, Kato, Kern River, Laguna, Luiseno, Maidu Mechoopda, Mattole, Miwok, Pomo, Salinan, Serrano, Shasta, Taino, Taos Pueblo, Walaki, Wappo, Wintun, Yani, Yokuts, Yuki.

Northwest tribes
Alsea, Bella Bella, Chehalis, Chinook, Comox, Coos, Cowichan, Cowlitz, Haidia, Kalapooia, Karok, Kwakiutl, Kwalhioqua, Lummi, Makah, Nootka, Quileute, Quinaielt, Salish, Siuslaw, Skagit, Takelma, Tilamook, Tingit, Tolowa, Tsimshian, Tutuni, Twana, Umpqua, Wasco, Wiyut, Yurok.

Subarctic/Arctic tribes
Aleut, Beaver, Beothuk, Carrier, Cree, Chipewyan, Gwich'in, Ingalik, Innu, Inuit, Kutchin, Metis, Montagnais, Naskapi, Slavey.

WHAT'S IN A NAME?

Most of the tribal names you see on these pages mean the same thing – "the people", "us", or "the humans" – in the language spoken by the people of the tribes. Since tribes spoke wildly different languages, some people developed expressive gestures for a tribal name. On the Plains, for example, a slashing motion across the neck stood for the Sioux, while running the index finger under the nose was the sign-language "word" for the Nez Perce tribe.

NATIVE AMERICAN GLOSSARY

Adobe Clay bricks used by some tribes in the Southwest to construct buildings.

Alaska Native A term to describe the native peoples of the state of Alaska.

Appaloosa A breed of horse with black and white markings, bred by the Nez Perce.

Awl A pointed tool used for making holes in leather or wood.

Buckskin A type of soft leather made from the skin of a deer.

Calumet A long-stemmed pipe smoked by Native Americans as a token of peace.

Chickee A Seminole house built on stilts, with open sides and a thatched roof.

Chief The head or leader of a tribe, respected for his wisdom, experience, and sense of honor. A tribe might have one or many chiefs.

Chunkey A stick-throwing game popular in the Southeast.

Clan A group of tribe members with a common ancestor.

Confederation A political alliance between two or more tribes.

Coup A particular act of daring or bravery, especially in warfare. Warriors who counted coup were rewarded with eagle feathers.

Culture The customs and beliefs that shape a group of people's way of life.

Dugout A canoe made by setting a log on fire, then digging out the charred insides.

Homeland The original territory of a tribe.

Ice Age A period of geological time when large parts of the Earth were covered by glaciers.

Igloo A dome-shaped Inuit house made of blocks of ice.

Indian One name for the native peoples of North America, also known as Native Americans.

Inuit The native peoples of the Arctic.

Kachina In Pueblo folklore, a helpful spirit, represented by a doll or a costumed dancer.

Kayak A one-person canoe made of animal skins stretched over a wooden frame.

Kiva An underground room where Pueblo people held important ceremonies.

Longhouse A barn-shaped, multi-family Iroquois dwelling made from saplings covered in bark shingles.

Maize Another name for corn.

Missionary A person who wants to convert other people to his or her own religion.

Mission A religious centre where missionaries try to convert native peoples to their religion.

Moccasin A Native American shoe, made of soft leather.

Native American A term to describe the native peoples of the United States, popular since the 1960s.

Native Canadian A term to describe the native peoples of Canada – Indian, Inuit, or Metis.

Pemmican A high-energy, easy-to-carry food made of dried meat, fat, and berries pounded together.

Piki A bread made from ground corn which was a staple of the Southwestern diet.

Pit house A dwelling made in a hole or cavity in the ground.

Potlatch An important ceremony among Northwestern tribes, in which the host gave away lavish gifts and food to his or her guests.

Powwow A festival where different tribes gather to sing, dance, and celebrate their heritage.

Pueblo The clay-walled, multi-family dwelling built by the Pueblo people.

Quillwork The use of porcupine quill embroidery to decorate clothes and objects.

Rawhide Tough, untanned animal skins.

Removal The policy of the US government that forced Southeastern tribes to leave their homelands and relocate to lands west of the Mississippi River.

Reservation An area of land set aside by the government for the sole use of a recognized tribe.

Shaman A male or female religious leader, who also used medicines to heal the sick.

Sweat lodge A dome-shaped structure of bent sticks covered in animal hides and heated with steam. People went there to be cleansed and prepared for religious ceremonies.

Tepee A cone-shaped house made of animal skins over a pole framework, used by Plains people. Also known as a tipi.

Totem pole A tall sculpture made by natives of the Northwest, by carving animals, humans, and spirits into trees.

Trail of Tears The 1838 relocation of the Cherokee from their homes in the Southeast to a reservation west of the Mississippi River.

Travois A carrying device made of a wooden platform suspended between two poles. The travois was dragged by a dog or horse.

Treaty A written agreement between two nations (for example, the US government and a Native American tribe)

Tribe A group of people with the same language, customs, and religious beliefs, who lived under one or more leaders called chiefs.

Tribal council In Native American government, a meeting of the leaders of a tribe.

Wampum Small purple and white seashells that were used to keep tribal records and as a form of money.

Wikiup An oval-shaped, portable shelter made of sticks and brush.

Wigwam A cone-shaped house made of saplings covered with grass or bark mats.

Wounded Knee The site of a 1890 massacre of about 300 Sioux and Cheyenne people by US troops.

Yucca A white-flowered plant of the agave family, with stiff, sword-shaped leaves.

NATIVE AMERICAN WEBSITES

www.ncai.org
The oldest and largest national political organization serves the needs of more than 250 Native American and Alaskan Native tribes.

www.narf.org
An organization that seeks to improve the lives of Native Americans through developing Indian law and educating the public about native rights, laws, and issues.

www.abo-peoples.org
Established to represent the interests of Metis and non-treaty tribes throughout Canada.

www.inac.gc.ca
An agency established to help aboriginal Canadians access federal programs and services, with lots of cool info in the Kids' Stop.

www.500Nations.com
Native American places to go, things to do, and people to meet.

www.gatheringofnations.com
Founded to promote Native American culture and tradition. Tons of information and brilliant pictures of powwows.

www.indianvillage.com
A site dedicated to Native American culture and trade, with a calendar of events, on-line shopping, and tons of links to tribal web sites, museums, and other sources of information.

www.nativeculture.com
A gateway to Native American resources on the internet. One of the best places on the Web to find out about Native Americans.

www.nativetech.org
A brilliant web site focusing on the art and technology of the people of the Eastern Woodlands, with cool interactive games, a peek inside a wigwam, and tons of recipes.

www.thePeoplesPaths.net
Pathways to Native American web sites, message boards, live chats, archived articles, museums, and much more.

www.hanksville.org/NAresources
A giant index of Native American resources on the internet.

Books and more

www.nmnh.si.edu/antro/outreach/Indbibl
From the Smithsonian Institution, an excellent list of recommended books, divided by culture area.

www.negia.net/~linda/NACSbooks.html
A guide to books and videos recommended by the NACS .

www.nativeauthors.com
On-line catalogue of work by Native American poets, writers, historians, storytellers, and performers.

www.firstperspective.ca
A monthly on-line news magazine for the native peoples of Canada, including listings for powwows and other events.

www.indiancountry.com
Stories and issues that matter to Native Americans.

www.nativetelecom.org
Listen to live Native American radio, or dip into the words and music from the American Indian Radio on Satellite (AIROS) network.

www.redinkmagazine.org
A magazine that features contemporary Native American literature, photography, and artwork as well as educational articles.

http://collections.ic.gc.ca
An amazing collection of web site links and on-line educational resources celebrating the history of Canada and its native people.

www.icom.org/vlmp
The quickest way to visit Native American museum collections without ever leaving your chair.

http://memory.loc.gov/
The gateway to the Library of Congress's collection of photographs, prints, and documents relating to Native American history.

www.nmai.si.edu
Try an on-line visit to the National Museum of the American Indian, part of the Smithsonian Institution. You'll find great links to hundreds of web sites. The museum is scheduled to open in Washington, D.C. in 2003.

www.si.edu
Browse the on-line collections of the Smithsonian Institution to find Native American artefacts, or try a virtual tour of the museum.

INDEX

A

ancestors 10, 13
anoraks 83
Apache people 68, 70, 71, 73
Appaloosa horse 66
Arctic 82–84
arts and crafts 38–43
aspirin 17

B

bags 46, 64
baskets 38–39, 51, 63, 73, 75
beads 40, 57–58
black drink 53
blankets 40, 41, 73
boats 31, 76, 84
boots 70
buckskin 48, 57
buffalo 26, 54–56, 59, 66

C

calendar sticks 73
California 74–77
calumets 34, 35
candlefish 27–28
canoes 31, 46, 47, 76, 84
carvings 43, 80
celebrations 52, 53, 59, 61
ceremonies 15–17, 20–21, 51, 72, 80–81
Cherokee people 33, 51, 53
chickees 51
chiefs 25, 34, 44, 51, 79
children 18–20, 23, 52, 63, 66
clans 23, 51

clothes 25, 53, 83
    bark 25, 62, 80, 81
    beadwork 57–58
    ceremonial 19, 25, 65, 81
    cotton 70–71
    fur 62, 74
    skin 25, 47–48, 57, 62, 66, 70, 74
cooking 24
corn 12, 24, 28, 47, 51, 53, 71
cotton 40, 70, 71, 73
councils 50, 58–59
cradleboards 63
crafts 38–43
crops 12, 28, 51, 71
culture areas 12–13
    Arctic 82–84
    California 74–77
    Great Basin 60–63
    Northeastern 44–49
    Northwest 78–81
    Plains 54–59
    Plateau 64–67
    Southeast 50–53
    Southwest 68–73
Custer, General 59

D

daily life 26–33
Dakota people 36, 56, 58, 59
dances 35, 51, 52, 59, 72, 80
desert 68–73
disease 37, 49, 67, 77, 81
dogs 11, 31

E, F

Europeans 32, 36–37, 43, 49, 81, 84

explorers 67, 73
families 18–23
farming 28, 51, 71
fishing 27, 47, 61, 64, 80
food 24, 26–28, 61–62, 64, 80, 84
    acorns 74–76
    cornmeal 47, 71
    pemmican 55
    succotash 47
forests 44–49, 78
furs 62, 63, 74, 84

G

games 20, 30, 51
gardens 47
Geronimo, Chief 73
gold 63, 73, 77
Great Council 45
Green Corn Festival 52, 53
guns 59

H

hair 20, 25, 70, 71
hats 66, 80
headdress 25, 58
hides 47, 55, 56, 66, 71
hogans 70
Hopi people 40, 70, 72
horses 20, 55, 63, 66
houses 24, 51
    earth lodges 22, 57
    igloos 82–83
    log cabins 45, 78
    longhouses 23, 45–46
    pit houses 66, 74
    pueblos 68–70
    tepees 42, 56-57, 70, 82
    temporary 11, 24, 61

wigwams 21, 45
housework 23, 30, 53
hunter-gatherers 10–11,
    24, 64, 71
hunting 20, 26–27, 62,
    84
    buffalo 54–55
    on horseback 63, 66
    mammoths 10–11
    whales 80

I,J

Ice Age 9–10, 12
igloos 24, 82–83
Inuit people 43, 82
Iroquois people 23,
    44–45, 47, 48
jewellery 25, 40, 80

K

kachinas 72
kayaks 84
kivas 70

L

lamps 83
land bridge 10, 12
languages 32–33, 44,
    68
learning 18
Lewis and Clark 67
Little Bighorn 59
looms 71, 73

M

mammoths 9, 10, 26
marriage 21–23, 52,
    71
masks 16, 43, 80, 81
medicine 16–17
medicine men 16
missionaries 17, 73,
    77
moccasins 48, 57, 62,
    70–71
money 32, 76–77
Mound Builders 50
music 16

N

Navajo people 41, 42,
    43, 68, 70, 71, 73
Nez Perce people 64,
    66
Nootka people 80

P

painting 42–43, 56, 78
peace councils 58
peace pipes 34, 35, 59
pictograms 33, 43
pine nuts 61
pipes 14, 34, 35
Plains people 15, 28,
    30, 33, 42, 54–59
play 20, 30, 63
potatoes 28
potlatch 81
pottery 39, 73
prairies 54, 59
Pueblo peoples 40, 43,
    68–73

Q,R

quills 40, 57
rattlesnakes 61
religion 14–17, 43,
    59, 72
reservations 37, 53,
    59
roaming tribes 11,
    60–67, 82

S

Sacagawea 67
saddles 56
salmon 64, 80
sand paintings 43
scalps 36, 52
scratching 52
seals 84
Sequoyah 33
shamans 15, 16–17, 43
shinny 30
Siberia 10
sign language 33

slaves 79
sleds 31
society 34, 51, 79
spirits 14–17, 39, 72
stories 13, 18, 33,
    48–49
Sun Dance 59

T

tepees 42, 56–57, 70,
    82
tobacco 17, 28
tomols 76
tools 28, 43
totem poles 78-79
toys 18, 20, 53, 63
trading 32, 38, 43,
    49, 76–77, 81, 84
Trail of Tears 53
transport 31, 46, 60
travois 31, 60
tribal lands 34, 37
tribes 12, 34
tule mats 74

U,V

US Army 59
US government 37, 59
villages 50–51, 60,
    65–66, 68–70, 78
vision quest 15

W

wampum 43, 48–49
war 34-37, 49, 58, 59,
    67, 73
war clubs 36, 43, 45,
    67
war dance 35
weapons 10, 11, 27,
    36, 46, 66, 67
weaving 39, 40–41, 42,
    46, 66, 74
whales 80, 84
wigwams 21, 45, 82
wood 45, 46
Wounded Knee 59
writing 33, 43

CREDITS

Dorling Kindersley would like to thank:
Almudena Diaz and Nomazwe Modonko for DTP assistance, Sally Hamilton the Picture Librarian, and Chris Bernstein for the index.

Additional photography by: Peter Chadwick, Lynton Gardiner, James Stevenson, and Tina Chambers.

Artworks by John Woodcock.

Special thanks to the American Museum of Natural History.